The Seven Traits of a Highly Successful Single Parent

By Paula Love Clark

Disclaimer

This book is designed to provide information and motivation to our readers. It is sold with the understanding that the author and publisher are not engaged to render any type of psychological, legal, or any other kind of professional advice. The content is the sole expression and opinion of its author. Neither the publisher nor the individual author(s) shall be liable for any physical, psychological, emotional, financial, or commercial damages, including, but not limited to, special, incidental, consequential or other damages. Our views and rights are the same: You are responsible for your own choices, actions, and results.

The content of the book is solely written by the author.

DVG STAR Publishing are not liable for the content of the book.

Published by DVG STAR PUBLISHING

www.dvgstar.com

email us at info@dvgstar.com

ISBN: 1-912547-42-2
ISBN-13: 978-1-912547-42-5

DEDICATION

To Harriet, Lauren and Zac. You inspire me to become the best version of myself every single day. Love Mama x

CONTENTS

'We delight in the beauty of the butterfly but rarely admit the changes it has gone through to achieve that beauty.'

~ Maya Angelou

'If you do what you have always done, you'll get what you've always gotten.'

~ Tony Robbins

INTRODUCTION:
From Jelly Bean to Rock Star Queen

I am writing this book because of all the men and women who have asked me to. This isn't a book just for single parents, but for everyone who wants to create a better life for themselves by taking some simple steps.

I am writing as a single parent. I have survived a lot of challenges, but I came back fighting, stronger and more successful. Quite simply, my life has been one long series of lessons learned the hardest of ways. These lessons and experiences have thus provided the material for this book.

I ask you, have you sometimes been so flattened by life that you didn't think you could ever get back up? Well, that's how I felt many times in my life. From being made homeless at eighteen, having my career path changed by trauma, to an increasingly unhappy marriage where I became lost, to losing my mother in my early thirties. It's been a hell of a ride!

And then the last three years: the challenge of transitioning from mud and fog toward clarity, power and purposeful productivity.

Are you in that space now? Feeling as if life couldn't get any worse or that you are so stuck you cannot see a way out of your situation? I hear you, because I have been there on many occasions. But that is a mindset to defeat every bit as

1

much as the slings and arrows that came your way in its very foundation.

This book is particularly for you. As a single parent for the past six years and a working single parent for the past five of those, the struggle is real. My hope is that you take something from this book, whether it's a word, a sentence, an experience or perhaps a plan for your own life, that may help you in your own life situation.

So who am I? Let's take you back to the beginning...

My challenges began almost immediately from very humble beginnings. I was number four of five girls. My father wanted a boy and kept trying. I think he pretty much gave up on us after the third girl. My mother struggled during pregnancy and should have stopped at number two or three. She didn't really have a choice.

That was her understanding, anyway. She was married at sixteen and having her first child at seventeen. Her mother, riddled with her own challenges, rejected her from early on and either through choice or circumstance, never delivered the type of love and nurture my mother deserved and needed. Having a strong, independent voice had never been an option for my mother growing up. She had a hell of a life, literally. That is her story, though, and in her memory, it isn't mine to tell.

My own childhood memories are pretty bleak and filled with a sense of loneliness and neglect. My father was an angry man: selfish, mean-spirited and a narcissist.

Life as his child was not a fun experience, although there were some flickering moments of laughter and happiness. But the pervading memory was a mother who was lost; a slave in herself.

So I write this book as much for women like her, as for women like myself and my sisters. We are all victims and we are all survivors. The difference is that some choose to exist in a victim mentality, whilst others do the hard work to become survivors and ultimately thrive. My heart goes out to both types. The choice for a person to remain as they are because of fear of change, or to shift one's perspective in order for change to occur, are both full of challenge. Choice is key. One can only play the hand they are dealt. I am enabling you to reshuffle the cards, even if you then choose to retreat and never play the table.

Let's fast forward in my own potted bio. Marriage. I should have walked away but stayed far too long, causing us both so much pain. After my marriage, my next relationship wasn't right for me, despite being beautiful, healing and lesson giving. I should have walked away then also, but I didn't. I wasn't ready to let go, yet also not ready to be in that relationship.

In my marriage, being a Christian who believed one made their bed and must lie in it, I was waiting for permission. I didn't know that at the time of course, but I was. When permission finally came (from a doctor treating my lower back pain), I knew it was the right thing to do. In the relationship, I wasn't strong enough after the marriage; I rushed into falling for someone, but he was just a healing lesson, not the long-term person for me. I should have let go; I should have given myself permission. Instead, he walked and my childhood fear and pain of rejection reared its ugly head.

In both cases, I was stuck in fear - fear of the outcome of my decision, fear of being alone, fear of loss. Fear is a bugger. It really is. It can hold us back and prevent us from living a free and fulfilling life. It's such a huge deal in most of our lives, that I have written a whole chapter on it in this book.

I believe that only when one can truly let go of the things that debilitate and imprison one's heart and soul internally, can one really start to live the life of their dreams.

This isn't about materialistic wealth, but inner happiness. You could be the CEO of a multi-million pound/dollar business, yet be wracked by feelings of shame, guilt and insecurity. That said, once again I stress this is about OPTIONS! Sure, you might not make a million, but knowing one's limitations is NOT the same as shying from ambition. Do not be held back by being held back. Try, test, learn, expand, move ahead. Be the very best version of yourself by first isolating the worst, be it a childhood memory or relationship/career setback. Redefine your focus and thereby your freedom to realise dreams.

What about those women in a loveless marriage, an abusive relationship, or those who feel professionally unfulfilled? To the outside world looking in, their lives might seem perfect by the image they put across externally. Such an individual might portray snapshots on social media that depict a sorted, happy, fulfilled individual having a wonderful life. They might turn up to the school gate with a lipstick smile and a swish of newly washed hair, whilst you might have just about managed to sling on tracksuit bottoms, trainers and a flick of lip balm for your dry lips. Or they might live in a huge mansion, drive an expensive car and enjoy luxurious holidays. All valid reasons for the comparison to your own life; perhaps enhancing feelings of lack. Rarely will someone post their misery or their issues for others to view.

We tend to present the best of us to the onlooker. And the truth is, only we can make ourselves happy. That's the crux of it. Most self-help books will reiterate the same message: that we have inside us the power to choose how we live our lives, how we feel and the choices we make. Ultimately, how we feel is always our choice.

It's a sobering thought, right? That no amount of money, material possessions, perfect job or the love of another can truly tick our happy box? That job is ours alone. 'How?' I hear a collective voice cry out. 'How can I make myself happy? Especially when I feel the way I do right now?'

This book takes a look at that and provides some tools and tricks to help awaken the part that is lost within you. However, it is ultimately one's own choice. You can choose to be happy, choose to learn a new way of thinking, choose a fresh approach to your life, or not. It is that simple.

I am hoping you take this walk with me and try some of the tools from the box of tricks I have had to learn myself. Remember that I too lived as victim and then became a survivor. Now, having worked hard on developing myself, I am proud to call myself a 'thriver'.

I must point out that I am no psychologist, counsellor, practitioner or therapist. I am simply a woman who has survived. I am going to show you how I did it and impart to you the knowledge I have learned on my journey. Ultimately the end goal is to thrive, but if you make it to survivor, then rejoice in how far you have come. You so deserve that victory in your life. Survive + Thrive is your new mantra. I am just coaching you on its core tones.

That's where the Jelly Bean analogy comes in. That's the term I used with my first counsellor, post marriage breakdown, to describe how lost within myself I had become.

The conversation went something like this:

Counsellor – 'Tell me how you feel right now?'

Me – 'Like a Jelly Bean. You know, those small, funny shaped, chewy jelly sweets with a hard coating?'

Counsellor – 'A Jelly Bean? Wow, that's descriptive. Please describe what you mean?'

Me – 'I have become so small inside myself; so shrunken, so lost…like a tiny version of me in a shell. Like a Jelly Bean.'

Counsellor - 'And how does it feel to be like a Jelly Bean?'

Me – 'Awful. I want someone to reach inside and grab hold of me and pull me out of myself. I no longer want to be trapped inside me. I no longer want to be just a Jelly Bean.'

Case Study 1: Polly's Story

What wasn't destroyed by the raging fire was smoke damaged. What we wore at that moment was all we possessed. We walked away with our lives but little else. There were still so many questions. How did it start and why did it ravage our home with such intense power in such a short amount of time? Why were the internal doors open yet the front and back doors locked?

My sister and her husband took us in. She was not far past being a teenager herself and her two young boys took up all her love and energy. Her husband, unbeknown to us, was crippling their lives through the drink and an explosive anger; remnants of an equally explosive childhood. Yet they took us in, all four of us, despite their own needs. They placed a large double bed in their dining room where we slept – a mother and her young children.

They lived in a three bedroom council house at the very top of a large hill. It was quite a walk from the village and about a mile door to door from our burnt out house.

I remember that day so clearly – a blazing hot, early July day and only three days after the biggest trauma to affect my life so far. As my mother, my older and younger sister and I trudged up towards the house, the weight of the past three days reflected in our legs as well as in our hearts.

I think we were chatting, but I can't remember that exact detail or if so, what about. I did have the distinct feeling of shock and relief all mixed together; survivor feelings after immense trauma. I knew I was lucky to be alive, especially as I was the last person to be saved from the fire beneath my feet. When the fireman lifted me off the roof of our kitchen extension as the flames below me licked at the back door and the ceiling inches below, I literally saw my life like a movie scene played out before my eyes. It was seconds, but I saw it all.

It's true that they say your life flashes before your eyes. It's incredible to say that and survive.

However, my twelve year old girl thoughts were on the utter horror of wearing pyjama bottoms with a huge hole in between the crotch. My father's old bottoms and I just happened to be wearing them during this profound moment in my life. I had a thing for firemen then and for many, many years afterwards as a result of one of them being my saviour.

We escaped into my mother's best friend's house two doors up. She took us in that night. Though not my father, just us girls; my sisters, myself and my mum. Her daughter was also my friend and I was both full of relief and mortification that she saw my family's utter despairing moments. It's strange how some thoughts and emotions never leave you regardless of time or the accumulation of other memories and experiences.

We had reached halfway up the hill that July day, when a voice called from behind us. A familiar voice and one that dropped my heart down to an ocean depth. We all turned around to see him standing there, looking wretched and broken and in obvious inner torment.

"Take me back. Please. Please take me back?" We looked at our mother and each other. We knew. Just knew. She was broken beyond repair and strength had left her body and mind. All she could muster was a slow shake of her head whilst she held back tears.

So many questions to ask; so much doubt and confusion infused the air. But I knew. I knew that he couldn't come back. We wouldn't survive the next time.

He called out my name as he had on so many occasions. The same voice. The victim voice. I had always relented and begged my mother to not divorce him, to take him back. I always believed his promises that he would change, or that he would *take us on a holiday (he never had). I would feel sorry for him. After all, he was our father, right?*

'Please. Ask your mother...' I looked at him. I looked at this man I loved so much and yet also feared. This man that caused me to sleep sometimes with a carving knife under my pillow, placed there by a fearful mother who was sleeping next to me some nights. This man I called Daddy.

'Not this time, Daddy. Please go away and leave us alone,' I said. The voice was small but firm and a voice I had never heard before.

I watched as his face crumpled, as he knew it was the end of his controlling and manipulation. I watched him break again, as I had witnessed him break three nights ago when my mother said 'no more'. His mental breakdown the night of the fire stays etched in my forever memory bank.

We turned as a collective and started to walk away from him. An unspoken feminine display of strength against a wretched tyrant and bully whom we no longer feared, but still loved with all our hearts. I didn't look back. I couldn't. I was strong in the moment but not without heart, compassion or love for this man I had known all my life.

Hours later, we were at my sister's home watching tennis. I remember that Bjorn Borg was playing and we were all sitting in the living room having just finished tea. The knock at the door interrupted one of the best tennis matches I had ever watched. I had a feeling; a sick, eerie, pit of my gut feeling, that whoever was at the door was not bringing peace or good news.

I was right. Less than an hour after I had told my father to go away and leave us alone, he did just that. And he was never coming back.

He didn't mean to kill himself. It was a cry for help and to get my mother back as he had done so many times before. But he hadn't accounted for not eating for days and therefore not lining his gut. The tablets kicked in immediately and he unexpectedly died. I say unexpected, because our neighbour who heard his last words said he looked shocked before he passed.

At twelve years of age, I took the last words I spoke to him and hid them deep inside me until my marriage ended 35 years later. Unbeknown to me, I had secretly blamed myself for his death and forever since avoided confrontation or deliberately wanting to hurt someone. It took two years of counselling to help me let that lead balloon go. In my forties, I finally managed to deal with the guilt I held onto since age 12. Time does eventually heal wounds, even the deepest, most painful of hidden ones.

~ *Polly, dancer, writer and artist*

CHAPTER 1

THE SINGLE PARENT STUFF

Originally this book's title was going to be 'From Jelly Bean to Rockstar Queen' but a friend suggested it was too ambiguous. Yet that analogy was the reason I chose to write this book: for all those men and women who felt like a Jelly Bean inside themselves. The book is more than that, though. It's a self-help guide book for those who, like me, were completely flattened by life and want to figure out how to get up and back on their feet. I had a message that I wanted to share from all the knowledge I had acquired on my 'getting back up' journey and all the tools I had to learn in order for me to heal and re-build myself, hopefully into someone better than I was before all the knockdowns. I had to learn to be mentally tougher and more aware of the negative habits I unconsciously slipped back into time and time again. To learn new skills to enable me to react in different ways and to re-programme my mindset from negative and self-admonishing, to one of positive self-love and self-encouragement. I had to learn a new way of talking to myself, to think in new ways and to react differently.

However, at this point, it is was worth noting that I had just seen one business shrink to almost nothing and the other disappear. My part time job I couldn't do because of the effects of trauma. So I was really struggling, not just mentally with a low, anxious and negative mindset, but also financially. Throw in being a single parent and you can understand the level of my anxieties.

I have been criticised many times for referring to myself as being a single parent or single mum. Mainly married women or men remark that I am labelling myself and should not see myself as being different because I am a 'partner-unsupported parent'. I listened. I stopped referring to myself as such for a little while, but then issues of childcare and paying bills kept hitting home that I was indeed a single parent responsible for providing for my family and bringing home the dough!

For all you non-single parents out there, imagine not having your partner's income to support your own. Not having someone to watch over the children as they sleep whilst you attend an evening networking event or are working. Not having someone to collect the children after school or at closing time for nursery/after school clubs. Not having someone to take the kids to school so you can do a two hour commute to the city before the school day begins, in order for you just to get to work.

Not everyone has a parent, relative or friend to step in if a partner is not available. Not everyone has an ex-partner who can co-parent effectively to enable you to go out to work and earn a sufficient income. I know I didn't have any of those options. I could occasionally call on a friend or the kids' dad, but they also had commitments. It's a wakeup call to realise that you are not everyone's top support priority just because you have to work! However, some lone parent families do have support, mainly from a parent, and this allows them to work. I admire those grandparents who step in to help and would love it if all single parents had that option, but sadly that often isn't the case for many, including myself.

So you have to figure out a way to make it work. If, like me, you became a single parent without either employment

(I left my husband's limited company) or an existing business to rely on, then your options for work are much more limited. Indeed, most options available to enable a parent to work within school hours are either minimum working wage or close enough. If you worked every school day within school hours, there would not be enough income coming in to support your family. If you can do this and retain government support benefits like tax credits then you have a better chance of supporting the family. I know because I have been there and so have many of my friends.

So how are you going to get in a better financial place if these are your only options? If you cannot go to the City every day or commit yourself to a full time, well paid job because you cannot get around the childcare issue, then what do you do? Is the low paid employment option your only choice?

The answer simply is 'No'. There are alternative options available to you. However, results do not happen overnight and patience, focus and determination are qualities you will have to learn to adapt if, like in my case, they are not attributes you possess in great quantities! I am the most impatient person going, so believe me when I tell you that I have walked this path with stones in my boots. I wanted change without a doubt, but I made it so difficult for myself and often fought against the tide of change. Why? Because let's face it, change is so flipping hard to do! I am hoping that the skills and tips I have learned on my journey will make yours that little bit easier.

Before we take a look at some options for thinking outside of the box in terms of employment, self-employment, or re-training, let's take a look at some single parent statistics. It's quite an eye opener.

According to the single parent site Gingerbread, there are approximately 2.9 million lone parents in the UK alone

(Office For National Statistics 2019). That's almost a quarter of all families with dependent children, that is, children at home and under eighteen. Out of those single parents, according to the statistics I read, ninety per-cent are women and the average age of a single parent is thirty-nine. So, that means that most single parents are within working age and most are women.

What surprised me most, however, was that they formed almost a quarter of UK families with dependent children. That's a huge percentage of the working population who are single parents. When you think that with limited childcare support and lower paid job options, then there is a huge swath of the population who rely on additional government support. This is not true for all single parents, however, as many work in professional jobs and careers or have thriving businesses. I am focusing here on those single parents who, like me, have little support or no current well paid employment, business or career to rely on financially, but who desire to get to that place.

There is a place that single parents can get stuck in – that no man's land of the income trap: not earning enough keeps one in the low income threshold and often on benefits, yet going slightly over means losing government support and possibly ending up financially worse off. It's a sticky patch and if you are building a business or career, then it's an issue that may have to be addressed depending on one's circumstances.

I have had to deal with this myself and this is the time when you have to dig deep and remember your goals and focus on your vision. My main goal as a single parent has always been to be self-sufficient and provide for my family. It has not been an easy journey, which is why I want to share some of these traits I had to accumulate to achieve that. I think of them as my medals of single parent honour!

Before we delve into these traits, let's take a look at the general view society has adopted about single parents, particularly single mothers. We will call them stereotypes, and many of them are reflective of a portion of society, but since this is a self-help book, then let's not focus too much on the negative stereotype. Let's face it, there are many people who are incapable, for whatever reason, of changing their circumstances no matter what help is available to them. I must stress that I am not a socio economist, a researcher, a government official nor do I have any qualifications in social breakdown or social research. I am simply a 'been there, wore the tee shirt' single parent who struggled her way through the brambles of oppression, debt, feelings of failure, lack of support and a loss of self-belief. I came out the other end, albeit with bruises, but that saying is so true – 'What doesn't kill you makes you stronger'. Let's take a moment to reflect on these stereotypes so lovingly (joke) portrayed by the media and society as a whole.

Single Parent Stereotypes According to Society

1. Single parents are scum and suck the life out of the State's coffers
2. Single parents' children are neglected and delinquent
3. Single parents have 'broken' families
4. Single parents are all unemployed or on low income
5. Single parents are tracksuit/shell suit wearing slobs
6. Single parents are unhappy
7. Single parents are unintelligent
8. Single parents are bad parents
9. Single mums only get pregnant to get housed
10. Single mums are desperate for a partner
11. Single parents live in hardship and poverty
12. It's our fault we are single parents
13. Single parents have a lot of time on their hands if they are 'stay at home parents'
14. Single mums got the majority of the house/money from the marriage breakdown

15. Kids of single parents will grow up damaged and negatively affected, or repeat the mistakes of their parents
16. Single parents should be pitied
17. Single parents believe they are victims

These are just some I could find, but there are many more I am sure. In response to the above list, I will reiterate that we are not all the same and not everyone wants to become a better version of themselves regardless of their situation. These are just stereotypes. There are many single parents who possess some of the above characteristics, just as are there many married or co-habiting people and single people without children who do. Without doubt, society fails many people and there are countless who lack hope, ambition or a genuine desire for self-improvement. They may not be the ones who pick up this book.

My call out is for those who do have goals and dreams and who want a better life for themselves. Whether you are a single parent reading this book or not, there are ideas, tips and tools to help you reach up and out of the situation you presently find yourself in, mentally and physically. If you take away one word, one phrase, or one quote from this book that will help you to focus or to bring you closer to your goal or vision, then I have done the job I set out to do. Remember that I was broken, mentally trapped in a negative way of thinking, fearful, lacking in confidence and stuck in debt-fuelled anxiety. I have walked this path and I will walk you through the steps in this book and hope that it gives you something to take you forward to the next level in your journey.

Stereotypes aside, even wealthy, beautiful and successful people can end up as single parents, as well as those who faced financial and childcare challenges. History has shown that many single parents went on to achieve life changing accomplishments and some brought up genius children. The message is that if they could, then so can we!

1. Scientist Marie Curie brought up her two daughters alone after her husband was killed in an accident in 1906. She became a Nobel Prize winner for her work discovering the elements polonium and radium. One of her daughters also went on to co-win a Nobel Prize in chemistry with her husband for their work on radioactivity.

2. Author J.K. Rowling wrote her books whilst a poverty stricken single mother. She has been one of the most successful authors ever. She also became the president of Gingerbread, the single parents' organisation.

3. Pediatric Surgeon Dr Dana. Suskind, widowed mother of three, founded the Thirty Million Words Initiative to encourage mothers to talk frequently to their babies.

4. Mary Kay Ash, founder of American cosmetics company Mary Kay Cosmetics (1963), a phenomenally successful multi-level marketing business currently worth over $3.4 billion. Mary Kay Ash has three children.

5. Belva Ann Lockwood, American lawyer, activist and politician, was the first woman to run for president in 1888 and 1894. Widowed, she was forced to bring up her children alone. She didn't allow this to prevent her from pursuing her work.

6. Actress Michelle Williams, whose partner actor Heather Ledger tragically died in 2008, leaving her to bring up her daughter alone.

7. Charlize Theron adopted two children despite her relationship breaking down after the first adoption

8. Actress Angelina Jolie, divorced mum of six, three adopted

9. Actor Liam Neeson became a single dad after the sudden death of his beloved wife Natasha Richardson.

10. Dwayne Wade, NBA basketball player – two sons

Single parent quotes

'Being a single mother is twice the work, twice the stress and twice the tears, but also twice the hugs, twice the love and twice the pride.'

~ Author Unknown

'You make it work. You keep getting out of bed. Sometimes it's just because you know there's a cup of coffee downstairs.'

~ Michelle Williams, Actress

'I would say to any single parent feeling the weight of stereotype or stigmatization, that I am prouder of my years as a single mother than any part of my life.'

~ J.K. Rowling, Author

'I want to show the example that you can be a single mother and work and handle a lot of other things at the same time.'

~ Christina Milian, American Actress, Singer and Songwriter

'Being a working mother and a working single parent instils in you a sense of determination.'

~ Felicity Jones, English Actress

'I can make bacon, fry it up, braid some hair and catch the football game. All at the same time. I'm superman because I have to be. And it's the highest honour of my life. I'm proud to be a single dad.'

~ Anonymous

'Shout out to the single fathers that have also taken the role of the mother. They don't get appreciated enough for what they do.'

~ Anonymous

'The loves of my life are my children and my mother. I don't feel as if I need a man.'
~ Diane Keaton, Actress

'It's the only way of life I have known. I was raised by a single mom. I was told I couldn't have children, so every day I am kissing the sky with happiness.'
~ Padma Kashkimi, American Author, Actress, Model and Television Host

'Hell, even the President of the United States – four of them in fact – were raised by single mothers. Nevertheless, mention you're a single mom, and all-too-many of us still have to cut through a thick, gristly layer of stigma before we're given our proper due.'
~ Taraji. P. Henson, Actress and Author

'I'm most star struck by the people in the small town where I live. Especially single dads like me who are working five times as hard to raise their kids.'
~ Kid Rock, American Musician

My message to you, if you are a single mother or father reading this, is not to give up. Not to quit and not to give in to social pressure to be stuck in a financial situation that isn't making you happy. If you are able to, because I recognise that some people reading this book have other challenges and obstacles that make change more difficult, then do everything you can to fight the stigma of being a single parent.

My hope is that by reading this book, you will learn or be inspired, to find hope in your circumstances, and that it will encourage you to either keep going with your vision, or to begin a journey towards discovering one. In the words of the wonderful English writer C. S. Lewis,

'You can't go back and change the beginning, but you can start where you are and change the ending.'

Take these words with you into the following chapters and keep an open heart and mind, and let go of that which no longer serves you, opening the door to hope and possibility. If you are stuck, lost, struggling or looking for direction, I hope you find some wisdom in this book, along with some tools to take with you on a new journey.

If you are a fellow single parent and you are looking for inspiration for yourself, then know that I was flat on my face, got up, stood up, walked and then run. If I can, you can. In the words of the beautiful and versatile American actress Jane Fonda,

'It's never too late – never too late to start over, never too late to be happy.'

It is worth noting that whilst you may not be able to please everyone and you cannot be perfect, you can please yourself. You can be the best YOU and be a better parent; not despite that but because of it. One cannot inspire change in others if they have failed to make it in their own life.

If you are reading this, then you are hopefully interested in realising your best self and inspiring the next generation to do the same. The process of parenting is by no means an empirical science. But one constant fact is that it is never easy, no matter your walk of life: financial, social, political or philosophical. You will worry from the moment the baby is born until the day you die, and even then you'll probably worry from the next life!

There is no guidebook given to parents that says 'this is how you do it'. And I would not even pretend to write that book. But what this book can provide, and I hope it does, is a step-by-step, linear and logical guide to becoming the best possible you, as well as a dip in and out, quick read. It's there to remind you that you are not alone and at the same time, that parenting is a personal project. Success does not have to be measured by wealth or status, but by how well you are living your life by the standards you set and the vision you have for yourself. Your personal vision is key to knowing where you want to go, no matter how apparently insignificant that goal may be. It's your dream, so own it and chase it until you have it in your hand and living it.

Finally, remember that you are not your kids. You do not project onto them. Equally, do not buy the myth that your fun, your creativity, and your passion projects end with parenthood. Being a parent, especially single, means you just inherited the mantle of manager, influencer, disrupter and role model. BE that change. But remember to be it for YOU as well as those adorable kids.

'If I am not good to myself, how can I expect anyone
else to be good to me.'
~ Maya Angelou

Case Study 2: Single Parent Story

My name is Trisha, I'm now 49 years old and I became a single parent from the moment I said I was pregnant back in 2001!

I wasn't in a relationship; in fact, I had just come out of a long term one that totally broke my heart.

From that very moment, aged 30, knowing I had complications that may make it hard for me to conceive, I made up my mind that this may be my only opportunity.

The father didn't want to know from the moment I told him, he didn't consider my feelings and offered to pay for a private termination!

I then knew I was going to have to put on my big girl pants and become a strong, independent woman and survive this, even if there was no one there to help.

There were other complications. The father of my child was a part owner in a motorsport company that I had just joined a couple of months earlier to make a fresh start from my previous heartbreak. Every day I sat opposite my boss, which was him, and he could not look at me. He made my work life balance a living hell and yes I did go home every night and cry. The girls in the office never knew that he was the father. I lied to them about who it was and they would actively in office girl chat say how could anyone behave like this and not commit to their responsibilities. He heard every word and yet carried on as normal, and I kept up the pretence. To this day none of them know.

I went into protective mother mode and this was the start of my journey; I knew I could do this for the sake of my unborn child.

At almost full term, working with the man who was vile and who dismissed me, watching me grow with his child, my only option was to move away from my job in Oxfordshire to Surrey, and at 31 years old and heavily pregnant, move in with my parents!

My son arrived a week early. The bond was instant, as was the tiger mum in me; nothing and no one would get in the way of my baby boy. I realised then that I could make all the decisions; I didn't need to ask anyone else. I chose his name (Harrison) and I registered him. The father did not want to be on the birth certificate nor pay any maintenance.

It was tough, I will not lie. I was living with my parents who were amazing in every way. But being a 31 year old woman, you really do not want to be living with your folks.

Six months later, I got a job in a recruitment company that I used to work at part-time to support myself whilst my parents looked after my son, for which I am eternally grateful. Of course, my plan was to move out ASAP and the only way I could do this was to work very hard. I went into fight or flight mode and had my goal to work towards.

After 4 years of being at home, I finally had enough money to move out. I got another job, as there were difficulties in my recruitment job and I broke away to work in Travel and Tourism. I worked my socks off, but the money was not enough. However, I did meet someone there and things were starting to look up. I was extremely proud of my achievements and my goal setting, with my own house being my dream, and now I had met someone.

I was blinded by love and although I saw signs of him being jealous of my son due to the attention I gave him (now aged 6), I brushed it under the carpet thinking it would change, but it never did.

I had changed my job again to a much better paid part-time job, but it was a very male chauvinistic environment and although I stayed there for the money, I was unhappy in my job. I also knew there were underlying issues at home.

When my son was 10, I then fell pregnant with our daughter. Once again I thought this would change my partner, knowing he had a child of his own, but sadly it did not.

It was then that I knew something had to change. I had left the well-paid job to go on maternity leave, knowing full well I would not go back. Although I had a partner, I still had to work and it was then that I decided to start a business for myself and joined a little natural direct selling company called Tropic Skincare, which at the time was less than a year old. I thought if I enjoyed pampering myself as my little Zen world, then I could enjoy a business around what I like and throw myself in to it.

My partner never supported me; in fact he hated what I did and wanted me to get a 'proper job' where I would have to put the children in childcare, which financially I could not afford. I knew I had to make this business work and the fight or flight mode took over again.

I knew inside that I could do this from home and build my empire whilst supporting my children. I dug deep, and worked hard, long hours and late nights but I did it: I grew my business, my team, my social life and met the most amazing and inspiring women, who became my business family that both inspired and supported me.

I became stronger, tougher, confident, determined and brave.

The relationship was on its last legs; he duly admitted his jealousy of my son and that he could not let it go. I stood tall and gave him the choice to stay and make it work or go. He chose the latter, and there I was again, single with 2 children.

I was broken hearted but knew it was the right move. For the next 2 years, my now ex-partner and father of my daughter made my life a living hell with almost financial ruin and solicitors and court threats. I could do one of 2 things - curl into a ball and let everything I had built crumble around me (there were so many times I wanted to,) or I could throw myself into my family life and business, which is exactly what I did.

I cannot lie; it was one of the hardest times of my life and due to the stress, I got ill and needed a big operation. But the whole time I had my family and business in sight.

Never ever lose sight of your end goal; even if you take the long, winding route you WILL get there.

A turning point occurred after my illness and my ex became unwell too. I am so pleased to say that I braved it, got well and looked after him through this too.

So here I am today in very strange times, co-parenting in the middle of a COVID19 pandemic and lockdown, again trying to survive being self-employed.

I have a very successful natural Tropic Skincare business, which has now adapted to an online business with over 180 amazing ladies on my team.

I bought my gorgeous 17 year old son his first car recently, having never been supported by his dad. My daughter is now 7 and is so happy and lives in a unicorn, rainbow bubble world, which I wish I could jump into. Plus my ex and I now amicably communicate after 2 years of hell.

I have had highs and many lows definitely, but I have become stronger and much more determined. I look back at my journey from 30 to 49 years and now only see the positives:

I did a pregnancy all on my own
I bought a house by myself
I'm bringing up my two amazing children
I have successfully grown my skincare business from zero to almost at the top (that goal is in sight)
I've achieved trips of a lifetime incentives to Morocco, Finland, Mauritius, South Africa and my dream bucket list tick this year in January 2020 to Vietnam and Cambodia prior to COVID19.
I have made the most amazing group of lifetime friends whilst on my journey, from colleagues to amazing networking business women and customers and to real friends. Plus I have learned to decipher the real friendships from the fake ones.

To survive this journey called life, sometimes you have to fail a few times to work out how to succeed the next time. Be strong and believe in yourself; you are honestly not alone. Stand tall, and when life throws you those lemons, catch them and make lemonade.

*~ **Trisha Mayes, Executive Leader at Tropics Skincare and Single Mother of Two Incredible Children***

Case Study 3: Aly's Story – No Matter What Life Throws at You, Don't Give Up!

I had many aspirations and big dreams when I was younger. Being a single mum was not one of them. When I was six years old I wanted to sing and dance like Julie Andrews from the Sound of Music. When I was eight, I wanted to be a glamorous actress like Joan Collins on Dynasty, and when I was 12 I wanted to be an animal and marine biologist and save the world's animals and inspire others just like David Attenborough.

I had always seen myself as a free spirit, answering to no one and living life to the max, whilst indulging in self-sabotaging acts. I felt that my life had always been a struggle in one way or another and I had allowed myself to be stuck repeating the same pattern of cycles I had learnt from my parents. Bringing kids into the equation was never really a sensible option.

Tick list or not, having kids did become a reality for me at the age of 22, when I found myself pregnant with a boyfriend that I barely even liked most of the time.

This time, though, the self-fulfilling prophecy and cycle had left me with the biggest responsibility of my life, when in 2002, not long after my son's birth, I found myself choosing the single life after my partner was unfaithful.

But there I was, a single mum with two young kids. It was Give Up or Get Up!

I suddenly realized, actually there was no choice to make for me. Give Up was never going to be an option!

Friends and family rallied round as they do for the first week or so, as I allowed myself the luxury of wallowing in a little self-pity, but I knew sooner or later I would be doing it alone. I was always pretty tough and emotionally resilient, but I wondered how I was going to cope and manage with two little ones to add to the equation. I couldn't run away with a backpack this time. There was also a mortgage to pay, too.

I initially think that looking back, I was working on automatic, like I was in shock most of the time. Nights were the worst, when the kids were asleep and friends had gone home and I was at my most vulnerable; fully alone with just my own head to talk to me ... and they weren't always comforting conversations!

The days, however, kept me busy with a new baby and an older toddler at nursery. Going back to work wasn't an immediate option, and I realised the house needed to go. I certainly couldn't afford a mortgage on my own if I wasn't working!

My dad and I worked hard to decorate the whole place and presented it immaculately when the estate agents came round to value. I decided to put it on for £10k more than their valuation, much to their disapproval. I did the viewings myself and to their astonishment, the house sold over their estimate and I got an extra £7000 more than their valuation.

I paid the fees, lawyers and any bills and debts my ex-partner and I had, and we split the profit.

My life was mine again, and to be honest, it was exhilarating and exciting to wonder what the future held. I was glad I didn't give up! I knew I could find happiness again and I had my children, so I was content.

Days turned into weeks and those turned into months and by 2003 I had a new partner and a third child on the way and a nice house that I bought using the profit from the deposit from my house sale.

In 2004 we got married and baby number four was on its way!

Life looked good, but then disaster struck a week before my fourth child was born. My husband ended up being made a scapegoat by his company and we spent two years building a case to defend and fight in court. In that time he was temporarily barred from working in his industry and his drinking got worse.

So here I was with a 7 year old, a 3 year old hyperactive boy, an 18 month old and a newborn baby which I solely took on the care for, due to my husband being consumed only by his court case, or drinking himself to sleep.

I tried various jobs over two years, paying off chunks of mortgage where possible, but found it difficult to do that and do all the chores for four kids, such as bathing, bottles and feeds. I exhausted myself and it was to no avail, as we lost the house and in 2007 I was told I had 48 hours to get my stuff out my house, since it was no longer mine.

I was homeless with four kids: my eldest now 10 and the others 5, 3.5, and 2 years old.

I was offered a hostel placement a few days later, but I had to pay for it. It was filthy and there were bugs in the carpets. To rub salt into the wound, most of my furniture and belongings that had been stored in a friend's garage had been soaked and ruined by one of the worst floods the county had seen.

Other children from the neighbourhood teased my kids calling us 'gypos,' which my eldest at 10 found hard. I can't tell you the hurt I felt for my kids. I felt I had failed them again in the biggest way, and I wanted to give up, but I knew they needed me more than ever!

We endured the filth of the hostel for 6 months, until eventually I got offered a house in the next town. It wasn't in the most ideal place, but the house itself was nice, so I took it and was so grateful to be out of that hostel!

The joy was short lived as my dad was diagnosed with stage 4 terminal lung cancer just after we moved in, and just before he died, my husband told me that he had been unfaithful. My whole world fell apart and I hit rock bottom... again!

I wanted to give up again! How much more did I need to endure? But I knew I couldn't. My kids needed me. I needed me!

I realised I was going to be a single parent all over again! My marriage was over, even if my husband refused to move out! Life was tough living in the same house and I didn't want to argue because of the kids, but we did. I felt I was letting my kids down once again!

I had to request a house swap through my housing association to enable myself to be properly single again and have a new start with just myself on the lease. It took a couple of months, but once again I was officially a single mother, but this time with four kids.

I could so easily have let myself be swallowed by a big hole in the ground. I felt I had literally lost everything!

My house,
My nice furniture,
My dad,
My husband.

This was not what I had envisioned my life to be.

I thought the world was punishing me for my past carefree ways.
I thought the world hated me.

I thought I must be a bad person to be punished like this.
I thought that God, if he even existed, didn't care about me
I thought I was doomed forever.
I thought I would never trust anyone again.
I thought I was never going to find happiness.
I thought wrong.

Not straight away, but after some serious soul searching, I realised something really important in all of that loss. I NEVER gave up! No matter what life threw at me, I NEVER gave up!

And something else I learnt: happiness, success, joy, love, goodness, internal peace...it comes from within. I didn't need to seek it outside of myself. I was never going to find it from others.

It's about whether you come from a place of FEAR or LOVE.

You see, when I had my children, I realised what unconditional love was and I fought for them out of LOVE. That got me through everything. But I knew I had to do more, or I would keep repeating the same patterns and fighting those same fights, and then what would happen when my kids grew up and left home? Who would I fight for then?

The answer had to be ME. I realised there was only one way.
I had to let go of fear.
I had to go within.
I had to unconditionally love me too, then anything is possible!

Now I come from a place of LOVE ...and realise that giving up will NEVER be an option!

~ Aly Jones

CHAPTER 2

TRAIT 1: KNOW YOUR SPACE

'The desire to know your own soul will end all other desires.'
~ Rumi 13th Century Persian poet,
theologian, teacher and mystic

The Space You Are In

Before we embark on this journey together, take a moment to reflect on the physical space you occupy right now. Grab a pen and notepad. It will help you throughout this book. Right at this moment reading these lines, where are you? What are you sitting on? Are you in bed? Travelling on a bus, train or in a car? Perhaps you are at home, or in a coffee shop or a pub or restaurant? Where are you? Take a moment to breathe in, take a look around and gather in your surroundings. This is your physical space.

What about your mental space? Where is that? I'll give you a moment to reflect. If you are unsure what that means, let me tell you where I am right now as I sit and write this chapter.

Picture this – it's early Monday morning, a national bank

holiday. Today in England, the United Kingdom where I live, it will be very hot. It's the third weekend in August 2019 and it usually rains at this time of year. You will understand this description if you've ever visited London at the end of August. Usually at this point in the season, the lush summer leaves on the trees begin their rusting process as they detach from branches and float to the ground. Despite it being August, autumn hints at her return and summer creeps without fuss or ceremony out the backdoor. On departing, she shakes the sand off her flip-flops, the Pimms bottles return to the drinks cabinet and we all watch with grim despair as our tans fade and are hidden from view under jeans and sweaters.

Today in London, it's the annual Notting Hill Carnival, a vibrant music and cultural Caribbean party on the streets of West London. I have never been but it's on my wish list. Later I travel to London but not for the Carnival. I have a date and he may cancel. It's a first date and I know he may be nervous about meeting, since he says I am his first online date. He will not be my first, but he may probably be my last since I am exasperated with the online dating scene. I have a feeling; a niggling, nagging doubt in the back of my mind. The question keeps coming to me: 'Will he or won't he cancel?' And I know that I shouldn't be manifesting a negative answer to that or focusing on him cancelling just in case my thoughts bring it into reality. I know this and yet my mind still goes there. It's a protective barrier I have yet to entirely break down. It's all part of the letting go process, which I will talk more about in the coming pages. These are my head thoughts. Then there is my physical environment.

It is the fifth week of the school holidays and I have only one of my three children at home and she is asleep. She is fourteen and very much a teenager. Her friend is staying over. They will soon be up and mooching around the kitchen, creating disturbance and leaving a post-breakfast mess. Part of me lies in expectation, awaiting that awakening disturbance.

Then there's the physical, visual part of me. I am sitting in my bed shorts and tee shirt outside in the garden listening to the birds and the distant traffic whilst tapping on my laptop. The sun is bearable now, but it will soon be too hot to write outside. I am grateful that the ubiquitous, chattering neighbours in the house situated behind mine have decided to return inside their house. They are a loud family, who communicate by shouting and moaning at each other whilst in their garden. They have a new puppy. It keeps them in the garden even more. It drives me crazy often. I write inside a lot!

I am drinking a homemade fruit shake in an attempt to eat more cleanly since a summer of holidays and work trips have created a flabbier 'mummy tummy' than I previously owned. My thoughts flip to the will he/won't he date as I regard the drink and consider my tummy. It sits beside a notebook and pen I always keep with me. They all rest on a broken rattan table that my middle daughter put her foot through two days ago whilst attempting to clean the conservatory roof. It will be a while before the table is replaced since both funds and time are limited in my life at present.

Does this give you a picture of the physical space I am in? Take a moment to look around you now. What is your physical space?

What of my mental space, though? Already I have told you of two of my 'background thoughts' about the date this afternoon and the anticipated awakening of my daughter and friend. Throw in getting let down twice on the weekend for friendship dates, drama with my oldest daughter at a music festival, two consecutive early mornings for wedding make up jobs (I am a make-up artist by day), plus big work opportunities to consider, then you get an idea of where my head is.

However, this is just stuff and thoughts and work and family and hope and possibilities. My thoughts and considerations are mainly positive. I may get blown off for this date and even though I like the look of him, I will accept that he is not the guy for me and will move on and because I am hopeful, I will keep trusting that the right guy will come along at the right time. Or as everyone reminds me 'when I am not looking'. My eyes roll up at this point!

It has taken me a while to be like that. To feel like that: to trust the process. To let go of the *what ifs?* It has not been an easy journey and yes, I have learned the hard way and yes there have been many, many tears and cries out to God for help and wisdom and all of the anguish that comes with desperation.

This is the mental place I am talking about.

The future excites me. For the past eighteen months I have been building an international make up artistry business. It is now starting to pay a decent income. I am once again starting to breathe life back into my finances. I am an entrepreneur and I have in front of me two business ideas that require investment and consideration. My thoughts are positive about these options and I mentally acknowledge that despite physical evidence to the contrary, I already have that money. This is the practise of visualisation and if you are not familiar with it, don't panic, I will explain it later in the book.

Despite being out of my marriage for over five years and exasperated with the dating scene, I know that the right guy is coming to me soon. Thus, despite evidence to the contrary, I am in full trust that this guy will materialise in the future. No matter how many disappointments I experience, I know that they are all lessons I have needed to learn in order for me to become more mentally prepared to meet the right guy for me. And as for all the frogs and toads that may have hopped onto my path? Well...there are no mistakes, right? Actually, that reminds me of a strange incident that happened almost three years ago.

It was around eight o'clock on a Friday evening. I had settled my young son into bed and was tidying up the kitchen. I opened the side door to take the rubbish outside into the bins. I don't know what caused me to look down, but there on the step, was a huge frog, or it could have been a toad; I profess to not knowing the difference at the time! I stopped in my tracks and stared at this curious amphibian. I expected him to hop away out of fright, but instead he looked up at me and stayed put. I had to step over him to empty the contents of my arms into the recycling bin, all the while keeping half an eye on my doorstep guest. He did not move.

So I did what any woman without a partner on a Friday evening would do – I started to talk to him. Yep! I kid you not. My girls came out and asked me whom I was talking to and I showed them. Lots of teenage girl 'eeks' followed and the flight response took hold. One of them shouted back from behind the living room door that I should kiss him 'just in case he is a prince'.

I looked at the wee fella and he looked at me. His little

throat was gulping, as though he could see what I was about to do. I bent down and perched back on my heels. 'So, you could be my prince, eh?' I said to him gently, whilst also considering the real possibility that I had officially lost the plot. I knew my choices. This guy was not moving. What if he had been sent to me? What if he really was my prince? If he was, then I had to kiss him, but the likelihood of my doing so were pretty low. Apart from the fact that he would be slimy, could be poisonous (this is deep Surrey, England, so highly unlikely), and of course, the frog/toad had rights too! What a conundrum to face as a single woman with no other date option in my life.

So I compromised. I kissed the index finger on my right hand and placed it on his left cheek, making a lip smacking noise as I did so. I stood up, sighed and said goodbye. I told him that I hoped he would be back as a handsome prince resembling Gerard Butler and finally returned inside the house.

About half hour later when passing, I decided to open the door to 'just see'. There he sat, staring and gulping. I considered feeding him but wasn't sure what they ate, so thought nature would sort out his requirements. I said goodbye again and put him out of my head. In the morning I checked and he had gone. No prince has yet come knocking. A few rogues, chancers, players and a lot of a-holes, but alas, this middle aged queen has yet to meet a prince. Maybe as a queen, I should be praying for a king?? It was an interesting, weird, unusual and very memorable story to tell my future grandkids in years to come!

So, even though I am a single parent with a weak support structure and no prince or king around, I am doing okay. We have a house and a car and I feed my fussy, food intolerant children every day. There is food in the cupboard and the fridge and almost always, there are clean pants in their drawers (excuse the pun). I am healthy and actively fit and told I am attractive and blessed to look younger than I am. I have a few close friends and many acquaintances. So by all accounts, I am doing okay. In fact, I am thriving. My mental space is pretty positive.

However, if you asked me this very same question almost eighteen months ago, the story would be so different. In numerous ways I was a mess. I had no job and my once thriving online business was so decimated, that it was barely breathing. I had no regular income. No matter how many times I applied for just about anything that could cover my monthly outgoings, nothing materialised. The make-up work was slow and mostly unpaid, since I was still in the building process. I accepted anything that came up just for the experience, the connections or to build a portfolio. It was almost the end of the summer holidays and I had no money for days out with the kids. I was lost, alone and broken by trauma from the previous two years. I was desperate and I needed help.

Then help did come. It arrived in August 2018, in the form of a spiritual healer to re-knit my hurting soul and a life coach to realign the negative, victim mindset I had adopted.

I am writing this book because I know how it feels to 'not be in the right place'. So let's see where you are in your mental space right now. Take a few moments to answer the questions below in the exercise.

<u>EXERCISE 1</u>

At the beginning I suggested you have a small notepad and pen with you when you read this book. You don't have to, but it might help. When you finish a chapter, or indeed the book, having notes will help you look back at what you have written. You see, when you write something down, your subconscious mind knows this is a 'golden nugget' bit of wisdom for you and sometimes you may hit a home run with a 'BAM!' moment. Something you write down might be exactly the information you were searching for to help change your life/ turn it around/ pick yourself up and get back on your feet. However, you don't have to write notes or do the exercises. The choice is yours. You can always go back and re-do them later, or further down the line.

I have notes on every self-help book I have read. I glean so much information from them and often refer back to a chapter, a paragraph or a sentence that may be relevant to a moment in my life or a situation I am challenged by. Sometimes I look back and just read the relevant notes and other times I may re-read the book and add to my scribbles. Often the message from the books I read is similar, but because each author has written the book based on their own experiences and lessons, then how it is documented is different each time. Finding one that speaks your language and to you is key. Make notes in or about this book, or take a highlighter, pen or pencil and underline or highlight relevant words, sentences or statements. Quite often it's in the way we receive the message that the magic can happen.

Let me explain. I have heard the term 'golden nugget' many times in my life. However, it was only during a boot-camp training with an online business I was involved in a couple of years ago, that I was truly awakened to the realisation that an idea or concept could be a golden nugget. Now, whenever I read a book or listen to an Audible, podcast or YouTube video, I consciously look for the golden nugget bits of wisdom relevant to my life and my goals. Whether I am listening to a live speaker, an Audible, a podcast, a Ted Talk, online message, or if I am reading a book, I write down the golden nuggets that I know will help me in my own life.

Open your notebook. Write down the title of this book and Chapter One, Exercise One. Or use the space below to write down your answers.

1. Write down your present physical space as I documented mine to you.
2. Write down your background thoughts.
3. Write down your mental space.
4. Re-read what you have written. Understand where you are at in this moment.
5. Place this exercise to one side.
6. What brought you here? (Read the next few paragraphs before submitting this answer.)

Answers...

What Or Who Brought You Here?

This is a biggie. What brought you to my book? Something or someone brought you here. The actor Jim Carrey, in his monumental speech to the students of Maharishi University of Management in 2014, said this now famous sentence, 'Life doesn't happen to you, it happens FOR you.'

Your life and the journey of your life to this point brought us together. It wasn't a coincidence. You were meant to find this book. Just as I was meant to read all those books I read and listen to those speakers whose stories and messages I invited into my home. Two of these included the American speakers Lisa Nichols and Les Brown. They stood out for me and lit up my mind and soul with their positive, encouraging messages on YouTube. Unbeknown to her, Lisa Nichols once saved me from a very desperate moment. Yet it was no accident. I was meant to find her online and later have her message impact my life in a dramatic way.

At the end of November 2017, I was experiencing one of the lowest, most despairing moments of my life. I was broken into pieces mentally and crying on the kitchen floor. My kids were on sleepovers with friends. I was alone and lonely. It was one of those 'what's the point of my life?' moments.

I cried out to God for help. I knew I needed divine intervention of some kind. So I begged to a Higher Being, with my heart and soul wretched and starving for help. My email box pinged. It was a subscription message from Lisa Nichols. Without thinking, I clicked onto the video link attached to her email. It was one of hope and encouragement. I was taken two steps back from the edge of me. A flicker of hope indeed ignited inside and then another email pinged my inbox. My phone had my attention and was seemingly having a conversation with my pain. The next message was from a support group that I vaguely recalled being a part of. It was relevant to the trauma I was experiencing regarding a close family member. I found myself messaging back on the forum. I poured out my heart to these strangers. Then I sat back and let the pain of my anguish wash over me until it subsided to a calming numbness. My email pinged once again. Other parents were commenting and responding to my heartbreak post.

I was no longer alone. I belonged somewhere. I was part of a tribe of other people in similar heartbreak situations. This was the start of my healing process. Knowing that others also experienced a similar pain and that I did not have to go through this alone was both comforting and a relief.

That sense of belonging was the first step in the process of self-healing and reconnecting me to my purpose. From that point, it was all about learning to love myself and forgive my failings. Boy that was huge. During the eight months of intense trauma forced upon my family mid-2017, my two businesses imploded and I could not face the return to my part time employment. I had moved twice and was in increasing debt. My friendship groups and support network shrunk to a minimal existence and I had lost faith in almost every person and institution. It felt like everyone had walked away and in reality, most had. The friends who remained I am eternally grateful for.

Where I am today, is light years away from the space I found myself in over two years previous and nowhere close to where I was eighteen months ago. It is often said that we have to hit rock bottom before we find ourselves. And I was there. Yet I was saved and I got back onto my feet. I crawled at first, then got up and stood, where I remained standing, watchful, still and quiet for a long while. Soon I began to walk again, then step into a light canter, before learning to run again, where I am now. The marathons are coming; everything has a time and place and that time is coming soon for me. It's an analogy, of course, as I have no intention of running a blinking marathon. My body, with huge boobs, weak lower back and a pelvic floor that packed its bags after the third huge child, is not very compatible for long distance pounding on pavements! If this were a post on social media, I would be inserting the laughing face emoji several times here. Please feel free to use your imagination!

So what brought you here? What situation, circumstance, trauma, illness, loss, divorce, breakdown or any other life questioning, soul yearning, heart breaking experience, brought you to this place right now?

Add that answer as point number 6 at the end of the exercise you have just completed. See it, know it, feel the emotion of it; it all has relevance for the work we are going to explore together in this book. Step by step, hand in hand, I am going to help pull out the Jelly Bean you that may be trapped deep inside you. Let's give her/him some freedom, acknowledge her presence and build her up to become her bigger self.

Who Do You Say You Are?

Description of Mindset - Wikipedia

' In decision theory and general systems theory, a mindset is a set of assumptions, methods, or notations held by one or more people or groups of people. A mindset can also be seen as incident of a person's world view or philosophy of life.'

This is a tough one. When we are lost, broken or stuck, it can be difficult to know exactly who we are. In short, you are who you believe yourself to be. So who do you say you are?

For example, if you are facing empty nest syndrome, where your child for whatever reason leaves the family home, you may be sitting on the edge of your child's bed, smelling their teddy or pillow, or longingly fingering their baby album, whilst mascara runs rivers down your cheeks. I've been there. It's wretched. That sense of 'what do I do now?' That empty hole swirling your insides around; that sadness chewing you up over and over; the constant reminders that he/she has left and is no longer a child running amok in your home. Perhaps for the best part of eighteen years, you have dedicated your life to that child and it may feel like one moment you are nursing them in your arms, crying out for more sleep, and the next you are sitting in their grown up teenager bedroom and they are no longer living there. It hurts. Like flipping hell.

You cry. Then cry and cry some more. You mourn them. You crave the chaos of them; their noise, the nurture, the laughter and everything about your child. You even mourn the tough times. You crave them. But mostly, you feel the loss of your purpose. What the heck are you supposed to do with your life now?

Quite often, when the kids are with their father on his weekend or on holiday with him, I find myself wandering in circles trying to find something to do to occupy my emptiness. I soon fill it of course, but that feeling of someone or something missing in my life is crushing. I get it. In fact, in my poetry book, I wrote an ode on this called Empty Nest. Part of who I am now, part of the trauma of the past few years, part of my former brokenness, was poured out into this poem. It was written for other women, but at the centre is my heart.

EMPTY NEST by Paula Love Clark

I watch you pack, displace your strings
I yearn to hold your childish things.
The teddy from a babe you've clasped,
Left on bed; I hear my gasp.
'What?' you say and tut your teeth

I feel a rage that sits beneath
The motherly love I wear on face
Really this is such disgrace!

How can you go, after all this time?
The times we've shared that were yours and mine.
The puzzles and books, playdough and beads,
Pushing on swings and planting of seeds.

Baking cookies and painting pictures,
Shopping sprees and parents evening teachers.
Crying together at soppy films,
Driving you to practise, parties and things.

And now you are leaving your mother's arms,
Leaving me with your plastic charms.

I'm proud of you, I know you know.

Like a mantra on repeat I tell you so.

Mature and focused, goals to achieve,

Yet I really do not want you to leave.

Stay here with me and we'll figure it out.

I'll be your taxi when you shout.

I'll make you tea and iron your shirts

Listen to your stories and soothe when it hurts.

We'll go shopping, have coffees

And lunches out

Gossip and giggle. And I'll never shout.

Don't go. Please stay.

I scream inside.

I want you always by my side.

'I'm ready Mum! We've got to go.'

You say to me in words, tender, slow.

I know. I know. I know.

Even if you have never had a child, or your children are young, or have not left home, you probably have some inclination from the above, how it might feel to have a child leave the nest. It's that feeling that I am wishing to explore here.

So where do you go from this place as a parent? How do you fill that child shaped hole inside you?

Or what about other scenarios? Other reasons for feeling as you do other than parental loss? You've lost your job, got made redundant, or didn't get the promotion or position you worked so hard for? Lost your home, possessions or car to debt repossession? Your business has failed, you are in recovery from an addiction, or maybe it's your marriage or a relationship ending that brought you here? Perhaps even a serious illness or death has taken you off your feet and disrupted your once solid and known space? Or is as simple as losing belief in yourself? Have you lost hope?

There are so many reasons you picked up this book. You may be looking for some kind of guidance to help you in the midst of your struggle and challenges. Any of these reasons, or others I have not mentioned, can leave a person feeling lost, broken, flattened and in despair.

At this moment, ask yourself this one question – 'Who am I?'

What's your answer? Who do you say you are? Take a moment and write down your answer in the space below. Fill it with as many words as you can to describe you. If you don't want to see the words after this exercise, then use a pencil so you can erase them afterwards.

EXERCISE 2 : WHO DO I SAY I AM?

How Do You Feel?

When my marriage broke down I kept crying. That's completely normal, I know. Nobody would question my right to break down and mourn the loss of my relationship. It's what I was crying over that was interesting. I was crying for the lost, known space I occupied. After twenty-four years together and as a loyal Christian woman, I believed my life was mapped out until 'death us do part'; that is, until old age called time on one of us. I saw slippers and dressing gowns, grey hair, cups of tea and two armchairs in front of a burning log fire. If you've seen the kids' film *Up*, you will get it. If not, try watching it, and you will understand my headspace at the time.

My world stopped when my marriage ended. The given path to old age came to a crossroads, and for the first time in my relationship, I had numerous roads to take, since the one I was already on had just run out of road. I was forced to choose a new direction, but I was trapped in inertia. I found myself immobile; glancing up, around and in every other direction. There was no 'ahead' sign to follow any longer. That sign had disappeared. I was stuck. I had to acknowledge the loss of my 'guaranteed' future. I had to give up in my head, the future projection of us as an older couple and the picture of the future life I had painted in my mind. That was the most difficult part of the breakdown to mourn. It also meant that since I was no longer part of a couple, I suddenly occupied a different space in life as a single person. No longer wife, no longer partner, I felt out of place in so many ways.

Relationships changed and so did the way people perceived me. Invitations stopped. Gone were the family barbeques, dinner parties or any social engagements involving coupledom. I have decided that it takes a brave married woman to invite a single woman to any social gathering. Not because the single woman or single mother is a danger, but because it goes against the norm. It is more likely an unfaithful partner will go off with a younger woman or a married colleague/friend, than choose a single mother with little free time!

My feelings post marriage breakdown were along the lines of 'What do I do now?' and 'Who the heck am I?' I questioned myself over and over. I felt guilty for calling time on this partnership, despite it being the right call for many reasons. I felt lost as a woman, wife and to some extent, a mother. I was no longer in a parenting agreement as such and had to step up and out of that space. My choices became more critical as they impacted not just me, but also my children and our futures.

Let's not even go there with the challenges of changing lightbulbs, D.I.Y. or technology, none of which are my natural forte! Finding the new me, in this new space called singledom, was filled with untold adjustments and emotional pitfalls.

After my divorce, I discovered my purpose had shifted. This is a valuable perception. What I realised a few years ago was that some women tend to lose their individuality in marriage and family life. I did. This is true for some men also, but because most men continue to be the breadwinners (a generic perception that isn't true for all family setups), they retain a percentage of their individuality because of their work, job or career. Basically, they have a life outside of the marriage and home.

If you have been a working mother then this may apply to you less, but when the children leave home or separation/divorce hits, many women can lose their perspective on their purpose. Likewise, when death or loss happens to us.

One of the reasons I am writing this book is in memory of a good friend who succumbed to cancer two years ago, aged fifty-five. I miss her dearly. Hours before her passing, as I read her stories at her hospital bed from one of the uplifting *Chicken Soup for the Soul* books by Jack Canfield, I made a tearful promise that I would write this book and help others because of our journeys. She had struggled in so many ways and we made a pact together, months before her death, to write about how we had survived and overcome immense pain and trauma. We planned to give hope to others who were going through trauma of some kind. This book is a carry through of that promise.

Marcus Aurelius, Roman Emperor (161-180AD) stated,

'It is not death man should fear, but he should fear never beginning to live.'

Loss comes in other forms too. When a lover or partner walks away and leaves a huge hole in your life, this can be exceptionally painful. All that self-doubt and self-questioning, as well as the loss of them, is so debilitating and can have a huge effect on our confidence and self-belief. I have experienced this myself and my reaction was to hide my heart in a velvet box and keep it on a top shelf waiting for the right guy. I let it down recently and gingerly opened the box with a rusty key. I thought I found someone I could trust, but it turns out the timing still wasn't right for me. This time, however, I didn't return my heart to the box. I have put it firmly back into my chest where it can thrive and beat. Instead of waiting to give my love to a guy, **I gave that love to me.**

~~~~~~~~~~~

Whatever brought you here to this space, it has come with a bundle of feelings. To enable you to move forward, it helps to know exactly how you feel. Whatever the words are to describe those feelings, write them down. Write them here below. Pour it out on paper for your eyes to see how you feel. This may be the first time you have written down the emotions inside you. It can be scary and you may feel ridiculous, but put it all down. If you are angry, write any words that come up, and expletives are allowed; this is your book after all. Scrawl as many words as you want. Expunge them from the depths of you. Believe me, it works and it is all part of the healing and mindset change process.

'Even a strong woman needs a shoulder to lean on, someone who'll listen as tears roll down to her face, and remind her that no matter how far she's fallen, she'll get up again, stronger and wiser than before.'

~ Author Unknown

EXERCISE 3: I FEEL...

How do you feel? Write down as many words as you can think of. Don't hold back...

Broken But Not Unfixable

If you did the exercise, take a look at the words you wrote. How many of them are sad, unhappy or negative? Are there any positive, uplifting, happy descriptive words? If so, take a pen and underline them. Or perhaps there are a mixture depending on your circumstances? If you asked me eighteen months ago to write this list, there would have been mainly negative, sad feelings with a sprinkle of hope. Today, despite various challenges that still exist in my life, my words would be along the lines of 'trusting', 'hopeful', visionary', 'love myself', and 'going with the flow'. Of course I get down and have doubt and feel sad and disheartened, but these feelings are not the most powerful or overwhelming that sit within me on a day-to-day basis.

Over the past year I have taken the torn pieces of me, stitched them back together and used some pretty amazing magic thread. To be honest, it's not magic, but through adopting a different mindset, I changed how I perceived myself. As a result, it literally felt like a radical, thought transfusion had taken place inside and affected me in the deepest of ways. Have you wanted that to happen? Waiting for a fairy godmother to wave her wand and take away the desperation, the despair, depression, anxiety or the feelings of lack, loneliness and loss?

At one stage I despaired that I may not be fixable. I felt broken and full of cracks and holes and that at any moment, I would crumble like an ancient old pot. Then Richard, my life coach, sent me a post one day that enlightened me. It was a piece about a mosaic work of art being beautiful in the eyes of the world despite being made up of tiny, broken fragments.

This knowledge sparked a realisation in me that we are beautiful despite our cracks and imperfections. I had been so occupied beating myself up for my failures and shortcomings that I neglected to notice the beauty that already existed in me. We all have beauty in us, but we often forget to love that beauty. It could be a particular skill, a kindness we possess, our compassion, our generosity, our ability to say the right word at the right moment, or even just to give the best hugs to those that need them. These are all beautiful traits that are deeper than a perfect face or body.

'Don't tell me the moon is shining: show me the glint of light on broken glass.'

~ Anton Chekhov, Russian Playwright and Short-Story Writer

Loving ourselves is probably one of the hardest things we can do, yet love ourselves we must if we are to be truly free and be the best of us. I hear a collective 'No, I can't love myself. I'm not that vain. I'm not good enough, I'm useless, un-loveable; a failure'.

Forget that negative self-talk and look at it from this perspective: by demonstrating unconditional love for yourself, you are showing everyone else how to love you. The same is true for the reverse. Beat up on yourself and guess what? You are showing the way for others to beat up on you too!

If you've ever wondered where these low thoughts about yourself may have originated from, take a moment to reflect on this – we are all products of our childhood. And if your childhood was a negative experience, full of trauma or your parents were negative thinkers, then the likelihood is that you may have created a negative thinking habit developed from an early age. This is generic and not true of everyone's experience. The good news is, because this type of thinking is a habit, you can break this habit and change your mindset. First, you may have to do some work on your inner child.

'The wound is the place where the light enters you.'

~ Rumi

Inner Child

The inner child is the subconscious childlike part of ourselves that we carry with us from childhood through to our adult lives. It's the part of one's personality that reacts like a child, especially when faced with trauma, challenge or situations that trigger a negative memory. It's a subconscious part of oneself that is also known as the 'subpersonality'.

The inner child can at best be childlike and at worst, destructive, self- sabotaging, narcissist and self-loathing. So many mental health issues can be traced back to a negative relationship with one's inner child. There are many techniques, healings, workshops and counselling practises, created to help connect a person to their inner child and create healing for past hurts.

I have had to work to connect with my inner child over feelings of neglect and loneliness, stemming from my early childhood. I had to learn to acknowledge the pain of my inner child, visualise her in my mind, and ask for her forgiveness, whilst also acknowledging the source of the pain and loving on my inner child to reassure her that I understood and recognised her hurts.

This is incredibly powerful work. It helped me to connect with the neglected child within me and to visualise holding her hand so that she no longer felt vulnerable and lonely. When negative self-thoughts threaten to overrun me, I simply close my eyes and imagine holding this little me girl's hand and smiling and telling her she is loved and that I won't let her go.

So many of our insecurities, hang ups and negative traits such as anger, defensiveness, bitterness, low self-esteem and even addictions, can be traced back to having a poor relationships with our inner child. This is fascinating work, and I implore anyone struggling with issues from childhood to look up the inner child theory and how to heal from negative and destructive thought patterns and habits.

Another technique that works to connect with yourself is known as Mirror Work. This was devised by Louise Hay, founder of Hay House and a motivational author of many self-help books, including a book on this healing work called, 'Mirror Work: 21 Days to Heal Your Life'.

Louise Hay's method involved looking into the mirror and uplifting yourself with self-love and self-care praises. The work is there to re-connect with your inner self and to build self-love, as opposed to self-negativity.

Go ahead and try it. Sit in front of the mirror and look at yourself compassionately and with genuine love. How do you feel? That's the key part: how you feel? If your immediate feelings about yourself are negative, then a re-connection to your inner self is required. If you cannot look at yourself in the mirror and tell yourself how great you are, then how can you believe anyone else that says the same words? How many of us are self-depreciating when it comes to compliments? How often do we bat off a compliment with a self-depreciating remark, such as 'What this old dress?' It's a cliché yes, but it so perfectly describes what most of us, especially women, do when we receive a positive word, comment or appraisal. We knock it down and create something ugly or negative to replace it.

Women, let me tell you a little secret. Do you know that one of the most valuable things you can say to a man are these three words: 'I appreciate you.' Simple. Just as women adore being loved on and made to feel special, men meanwhile, love it when we appreciate them and the things they do for us. They also need compliments. Let's face it, we all do! But what if there is no one to do the complimenting? Then what? Well, that's when we have to take on the task ourselves.

Try the two exercises – the Inner Child and the Mirror Work. Read Louise Hay's books, including 'How to Heal Your Life'. Her work was insightful and helped changed millions of lives globally. This is time to change your life and there are countless tools, methods, techniques, books, online messages and practitioners to help you.

For now, try this: Go to the mirror if you can, or do this exercise wherever you are right now. Take a deep breath and as loud as your environment will allow (you can do it in your head if you really are unable to speak aloud, say if on a bus or train!), proclaim these words...

'I LOVE MYSELF. I LOVE MYSELF UNCONDITIONALLY. I AM FRICKING AWESOME!'

Have you done it? If so, how did it feel? Come on; be honest. Did you feel free? Amazing? Totally flipping awesome? Or perhaps it felt abnormal, terrifying, un-truthful, like you were seriously kidding yourself? Honestly, when I was first asked to say it, it wasn't achievable for me. I simply couldn't. I really didn't think I deserved to be let off the hook by declaring that I actually loved myself. No wonder I didn't feel loved back by the world in the space I was in a few years ago. I wasn't showing others around me how much I deserved to be loved on.

By changing the way you look at yourself, the things you look at change. These words, or similar, have been said by so many thinkers, authors and speakers and you will not just hear them from me, but many times along your developing journey. Bring it to the forefront of your consciousness right now, because it's true. When you start to love who you are then your life will start to change moment by moment. It may not happen overnight, but so gradually, that in months you may be unrecognisable from the person you are now. Watch as others around you will notice the changes. Love yourself like you are the only person in the world who could love you that much. This isn't an ego led, narcissistic view of yourself, but a loving of your inner self. If you are a parent, try to imagine how much you love your children, and then love yourself that much, if not more.

The pain and trauma of childbirth (don't worry, us women soon forget this part and often go on and have more), the sleepless nights, the toddler tantrums, the juggle of childcare and work, the crazy teenage years, the letting go when they leave home, the heartbreak of watching their hearts break. The list is endless. Yet despite all they do and the stress, anxiety, worry and frustration parents often experience, the love for a child is without limitations for most parents. There are always exceptions, of course. Take this love and quadruple and multiply it. This is the depth of love you should feel for yourself on a daily basis.

Still struggling with this concept of self-love? It's okay, we will go through the book and come back to it at the end. For now, write a number below, or someplace else you can reference, on a scale of 1-10, with 1 being lowest and 10 being highest, where you would place yourself at self-love.

EXERCISE 4: I LOVE MYSELF...

Score yourself a self-love mark between 1 – 10. 1 being lowest and 10 being highest.

Come back to this exercise at the end of the book and answer the question again.

Hopefully your self-love rating would have improved!

Chapter Summary

1. The space you are in. Recognising that our 'right now' space is as important to our growth as the place where we want to end up. Examining and journaling the spaces we currently occupy:

    - Your physical space

    - Your background thoughts

    - Your mental space

2. What brought you here? Understanding the impact life or a particular circumstance/situation has had on you and your response. How do you perceive yourself right now?

3. Who do you say you are? How you describe yourself affects your self-perception. You are who you say you are. You are what you think. There is power in the spoken word and in thought.

4. Your feelings. How are you feeling right now?
    - The acknowledgement of how you feel is key to the process of moving forward
    - Before change can take place, be aware of how your present circumstances are affecting your feelings about life and yourself

5. Broken but not unfixable.
    - Seeing the beauty in your fragmented space
    - The importance of self-love in your life
    - Loving who you are right now
    - Reconnecting with your inner self and your inner child

A final note on Chapter Two...that guy let me down. I sensed he would. Go figure! So I grabbed my laptop, my notepad and pen and my purse and sat in a pub and had a lovely time by myself. When you are your own best friend, you are never alone.

If you take away anything from this chapter, I hope it's the importance of knowing where you are, what brought you to that place and a desire to move forward. I love this ancient Chinese proverb about becoming a better version of you:

'The perfecting of one's self, is the fundamental basis of all moral development.'

#iamenough! And so are you!

Case Study 4: Divorce – Kate's Story

I remember it as though it were last night. I had just settled Dylan to sleep. John was late and he had promised to put Dylan to bed and finish the last chapter of the book that they'd been reading together. He worked in London and sometimes the trains cancelled so he was often late. I had this unhappy feeling inside me that I couldn't work out. I'd been anxious all day and just had this dull, sickening ache in my stomach. Something wasn't right. Truthfully, it hadn't been right for a long time, but my middle class, stiff upper lip attitude pushed it to one side.

In truth, I didn't want to face what I knew was coming.

Two hours after he was due home, I heard the click of the front door. I was in the living room nursing a cold cup of coffee, staring blankly at the TV with some programme that I couldn't focus on. I still can't recall what the hell I was watching. I remember jumping up with a mixture of relief and anger. I had sent him messages in the day he hadn't responded to and of course my overactive, anxious mind immediately flew to the worst conclusions. When the door clicked, at least I knew he was alive.

I remember that I called out his name and walked into the kitchen. 'John?' Weirdly, I can recall the sound of my voice. Kind of strangled and not like a sound I would normally make. He didn't answer, but I could hear him opening the fridge. I walked in to find him looking in the cutlery drawer for the bottle opener. He had his back to me and was holding a beer in his left hand.

I could feel the tension tingling in the room. I steadied myself against the side of a unit. He still hadn't acknowledged me, and the only sounds filling the air were the clanging of the cutlery in the drawer.

'It's by the sink,' I offered.

He thanked me. His words were so quiet and strange sounding. He stood with his back to me still as he opened the bottle. He took a swig, sighed deeply, then turned around. I will never forget the pained look on his face. In the twenty-one years of being together, I had never before seen him look so inwardly tortured.

'What is it? What's wrong?' I asked. But my gut knew what my head refused to. I couldn't move. I was stuck still on the spot.

'Kate. Sit down.' He gestured to the chairs at the kitchen table. 'We need to talk.'

I remember not being able to move. My feet had turned to stone, my legs to jelly and my heart was banging so loud in my chest I thought I was going to vomit. I wanted to scream at him. I knew what was coming, but my voice had left me. I pulled up a chair and sat.

For the next hour, he told me how unhappy he'd been for a long time; over two years, he said. He felt he was going through the motions of marriage and family life. He loved the kids but he'd fallen out of love with me and what he called 'the middle class humdrum'.

I asked him repeatedly if there was someone else. He kept saying no. I asked again and again. No. No. No. There wasn't anyone else. I wanted to believe him but a part of me wasn't sure. It just didn't make sense.

Then came the words every married person dreads. 'I want a divorce.'

I screamed then. I just remember shouting at him and at one stage hitting him. I was so angry. I cried and begged and sobbed. He held me tight at one stage, perhaps to stop me hitting him again, I can't remember. I had never hit him before and I hate the idea of domestic violence.

I could smell him. The aftershave I'd bought him for Christmas, the smell of beer and the commute. And another sweeter smell that was faint but distinct. The remnants of that smell have stayed with me to this day. At the time, I only sensed what I now know.

He moved out the next day. He'd already found a flat close to his work. There was no option for counselling or discussions, or sticking plasters on open sores; the decision was made. It was final and I got no say. That was the hardest part of all. I knew he wasn't happy but it was never openly said until that night and by then it was too late. I remember feeling intensely angry, not just for me but for the children. They were now part of a broken family and I had become a single parent overnight. How did that happen? How the hell did my life take that turn literally overnight?

And yes, he was having an affair and it was a younger, childless woman at work. The real cliché. My life had now become a flipping cliché. The man I loved and trusted, the man who said his vows to me all those years ago, who said he would never leave me. The father of my children and the source of the family income. Overnight he was gone, and into the arms of a younger woman. He faced me straight and lied over and over to my face that he wasn't seeing anyone and yet for months he had been shagging this woman all over the place. The stories I *have heard from a mutual friend whose husband works with him have utterly shocked me. I'm not sure I will ever be able to trust a man again. My world was broken and it can never go back to the safe place it was. Life is not and will never be the same.*

~ Kate, Surrey, Divorced Mum of Two

Case Study 5: The Break Up – Jason's Story

I met Alice on a dating app. Chat conversations went great, revealing that communication was definitely a strong suit for both of us. Within a week, we agreed we both wanted to meet each other and see if the connection through text would match in person. We had planned to meet for dinner, and as I walked towards the restaurant, she was walking there at the same time. I recognized her from afar and waited for her to walk up. Neither one of us knew what to do, how to greet each other, so we agreed to go inside. After a night of incredible conversation and many first kisses, we both knew we wanted to see each other again. Our third date ended up being Valentine's Day. We went to a club and listened to live jazz. We danced. We kissed. Oh, how we kissed. That night, we made love. The connection was so incredibly powerful. In the next couple of weeks, we continued to learn more about each other, and we met each other's friends. And then came the fall.

It came about as quickly as everything had happened in the first place. She told me she realised she wasn't as ready as she thought she was for dating and what we both seemed to be growing towards. She said she didn't feel any pressure from me, but it was pressure on herself. There was nothing wrong with me or between us, in fact, she said, things were amazing. Maybe too amazing. She said she realised that she hadn't done the kind of healing work on herself that I had done the previous year, and she needed time to herself to finally face it. And with that, she was gone.

We had only known each other a month, but the quick ending and the loss of what we had hit me in a way I didn't expect. It came after a lifetime of searching for a true partner, which resulted in a 23 year marriage to the wrong woman, a 2

½ year relationship with someone who I thought was my perfect match, and many dates with various women as I continually put myself out there in that search. I felt a profound sense of loss in the week afterward, but I believe it was far more than just for her.

I've always been fascinated by this idea ... was it better to have something truly powerful and meaningful with someone for a month, or even a week, or even one night, or would it be easier and better to have not known her at all? I kept wondering how many times you could find someone that you really click with, and how many times you could endure the loss of someone you really care about. How many times do so many people find themselves having to deal with that? Loss is an essential part of life, I've learned. It's how we handle it that matters.

My last words to Alice were, "Just being honest, I would really love it if you find your way back to me." Maybe one day she will. More than likely, she won't. But each day forward is a step towards what I've searched for all my life ... that person meant for me. My perfect match. The love of my life. For now, I settle in the warmth of what I was able to share with another human being on this journey, even if it was as brief and as fragile as a candle burning. We burned, for a time, and perhaps that fire might light again.

~ Jason, Filmmaker and Writer, Alabama, USA

CHAPTER 3

TRAIT 2: **KNOW YOUR SHAPE**

'Your thoughts shape your vision. You see what you choose to see.'
~ Anonymous

What Shape Are You?

Firstly, do not panic, this is not about your physical shape, so stop holding in your tummy right now and breathe out. Rest assured, there is no judgement in this book!

When I discuss shape, it's taking a good look at where you are right now in your mental space. Remember, we spoke about that earlier? What did you write? Go back and take a look, or if you did not write it down, then come up with a few words now.

Heartbroken, lost, distracted, empty, anxious, depressed, despairing, feeling like a failure, grieving, flattened? Eighteen months ago all of those words applied to me before my transformation. Throw in tearful, sad, lonely and generally feeling like crap, you may get a general picture of where I was at! It wasn't a very comfortable place. So how are you feeling? What is your 'mental state shape' right now? And more importantly, are you ready to change that shape?

Richard, my life coach, sent a post to me one day that went something like *'Your present situation is not your final destination.'* I remember reading this over and over, trying to comprehend that my life one day in the future, might be so very different than it was at that moment in time. Lost and broken, I struggled to see further than my own nose. The tomorrows looked as bleak as the present day and the yesterdays were filled with regret, sadness, anger and disappointments. Living in the past and worrying about the future created anxiety which meant the present moment was almost unbearable. Caught in this negative, anxiety fuelled thought process, I remained stagnant and desperately unhappy. I was in a dreadful mental and emotional shape.

One day I slumped to my knees and begged God to send me someone to help me escape from this tormented state. In wafted Richard with daily pinging messages on my phone and posts offering hope and positivity. I must admit that I pretty much ignored these messages at first. Then he sent one that grabbed my full attention. He'd been involved in a life altering and almost fatal accident and whilst trapped in his hospital bed, he saw a quote and thought of me. This was someone I only once communicated with via Facebook messages. *He had seen a quote and thought of me.* Initially my response messages to Richard were ones of sympathy and concern. Trust between us built and I opened up to him about how I was feeling, my situation and what had brought me to my present, broken state. He kept messaging and I responded with the odd quip, question or remark, or simply with gratitude. Until one day, I asked him a question that changed the dynamic of the correspondence.

'Why are you sending me these things? Why do you care?' I asked.

I cannot recall the exact words in his response, though I am sure Richard can, but it was something along the lines of 'Because you need me to.'

Looking back, I can see how the plea I put out and up reached Richard's heart. You may be as sceptical as I was, but it worked. Everything in me desired help and that energy went out and Richard's messages came back like a boomerang of energy; however, my throw out was in desperation and the return throw was one offering hope.

Since he could not speak or walk at that time, he messaged on his phone. One day, about a month after his accident, one of my many mournful, self-pitying, woeful, frustrated and displacement messages, must have triggered a response in him. He replied with a simple question, *'Ask yourself'*, he said, *'is what I am doing now getting me closer to where I want to be in the future?'* It's an adaptation of a famous quote by one of my favourite authors, Paulo Coehlo.

It stopped me in my tracks. I repeated it over and over to myself until I fully understood the meaning behind it. 'No!' I said aloud to myself one day not long after. It was a huge revelation to me. My language had been full of negative self-talk and yet I had pie in the sky ambitions. He hit a home run with that question.

Before I knew it, he had offered to take me on a healing journey to change my mindset. Was I in? Damn right I was, but really speaking, I was terrified of change. This quote really explains where I was and where I wanted to be:

'Why do you stay in prison when the door is so wide open?'
~ Rumi

What terrifies you? What are your fears? Let's take a closer look at fear and perhaps change your perception of it to relate to your life, because ultimately, if you don't change, nothing changes.

FEAR

'It is man's only enemy – fear of lack, fear of failure, fear of sickness, fear of loss and a feeling of insecurity on some plane.'
~ Florence Scovel Schinn, Artist, Illustrator and Author of The Game of Life and How to Win It.

Dictionary definition of **Fear...**

'an unpleasant emotion caused by the threat of danger or harm.'

Or how about this instead?

False
Evidence
Appearing
Real

The latter description is much more positive, don't you think? Fear isn't real; it simply feels like it. Let's delve deeper into this concept by taking a look at the word *FEAR*.

So what is fear, really? Fear is our mind reacting to a perceived threat to protect us from an imaginary negative outcome. So in reality, fear is in our thoughts; it isn't real. Let's sit with this a moment.

Think of something that terrifies you. One thing. It might be spiders, flying, open spaces, clowns, change, new environments, being alone, or even death. Whatever the fear is, it isn't real. It exists in our minds. Fear is simply a safety mechanism devised by our minds, imagining a negative outcome to something that might not even exist.

There are many names for fear: terror, fright, panic, alarm, foreboding, phobia. They can all create the same reaction within us if we give in to the fears - a fight, flight or freeze response.

Here is an example where I experienced intense fear just last night. I have always had a terror of spiders. This isn't unusual and it's one of the more common phobias. There is no reason for my fear of spiders, that I am consciously aware of, but when I see one, I go into a *freeze* response. If it's a big, black long legged one, I will scream and literally wet my pants! Ewww. My kids then have to step in and do the glass and envelope trick to remove it to stop Mother screaming and possibly having a heart attack. Basically, they have had to overcome their own fears of spiders since their dad and I spilt up.

Back to last night...my middle daughter had helped me decorate my room that day and we moved around some furniture and there were clothes and stuff on my bed. All the kids were on sleepovers that night, so I was alone in the house writing. I tidied these things away and began to make my bed with fresh linen. Something moved on my shoulder. I thought it was one of my long wavy hairs from my head, which were always falling out, so I brushed my shoulder towards the bed. It wasn't a strand of hair that fell onto the bed, but a HUGE black, chunky, long legged house spider. I screamed and screamed but wouldn't take my eyes off it. It was panicking and trying to escape, so I covered it with pillows and ran downstairs to get a glass and thick envelope.

Now at this point, I have to mention that not only was I on the phone with my seventeen year old daughter, but I had just started to write this chapter on fear and reading up on common fears. Did I subconsciously manifest a huge spider on my head? It wouldn't surprise me in the slightest.

So I was shaking with fear, with a glass in one hand and an envelope in the other and my phone attached to my left ear as my daughter calmly gave me instructions. *Put the glass over the spider, slide the envelope under the glass to trap the spider and throw it out the window.*

'Arrghh! I wish you were here. I don't want to do this!' I cried into the phone.

'Mum, stop being a wuss and face your fear and just do it,' came the sharp reply. How ironic, I thought. Here I am, writing a chapter on facing fears and I am facing my own. I placed the phone down but refused to let her go, so I put her on speaker.

'The window is closed!' I screamed into the phone. Panicking, with my heart beating like that drumming sound in the Jumanji film, I moved closer to the spider so I could open the window.

'Mum, just do it!' my daughter shouted back, laughing.

I swallowed hard. Without taking my eyes off the pile of pillows, which I hoped still contained the trapped arachnid, I leaned over the bed and opened the window. I then removed each pillow carefully. There were three. Each time my thoughts took me back to the sensation of the spider crawling on my shoulder, my arm and then seeing it land on the bed. The combination of my feelings and the impact of seeing the spider exacerbated the feelings of fear. With each pillow removal I screamed. Every time I thought of the spider, I screamed. Crazy right? Irrational, crazy, unexplained fear of a creature a third the size of my hand (it was big). I could hear my daughter laughing and admonishing me every time I yelled.

'Last pillow!' I cried out and screamed even louder when I finally saw it.

'Put the glass over it and slide the envelope underneath, then throw it out the window. Come on Mum, you can do this.'

I took a second to stare at this creature. I imagined huge eyes looking up at me and threatening to pounce. I spoke into my fears. *Okay Paula. You can do this. You have to. You are the only person here so you have no choice but to just do it!*

I placed the glass over the spider and watched as it desperately tried to escape. Shaking, I slid the envelope underneath, but it was a window envelope and the plastic window part got stuck on the glass. Yep...more screaming and pants wetting ensued. 'It's stuck. The envelope is stuuuuuckkkk!' I cried aloud. With my daughter's calm encouragement and without wanting to harm this creature, I managed to edge the glass and the spider backwards so I could effectively cover the bottom of the glass and conceal the spider's possible exit route. Then I carried them over to the open window and threw the spider into the bushes outside. I quickly slammed the window shut and breathed. I don't think I breathed a breath whilst executing that task.

Okay, so this wasn't particularly facing my fears as I screamed continuously and pretty much panicked throughout. My daughter kept me calm and I am so grateful to her. The 'facing my fears' part came in the going to sleep that night. After I made my bed and checked my slippers and underneath the bed, I decided I wouldn't avoid my bedroom. If this had happened with the kids in the house, I know I would have slept with one of them, in fear of that room now having transformed into a hotel for spiders.

Instead, I spoke calmly to myself: 'All is well. You are safe. You will sleep perfectly well tonight.'

And I did. Without hiding under the covers, without dreaming of spiders and without any terror whatsoever infecting my subconscious, I slept a beautiful sleep.

When my oldest daughter was going through a period of intense anxiety a few years ago, she developed extreme fears. They arrived from nowhere, and were completely irrational, increasing with each experience. They ranged from a fear of the deep sea, to heights, to bridges, clowns, enclosed spaces, flying, being surrounded by too many people, speaking in public and spiders. Yes, believe it or not, she was also scared of spiders.

As she developed coping skills for her anxiety, her fears diminished. The situation last night was a clear example of that. This summer, she swam in deep water, helped me drive over a very high bridge during our family trip to Spain (let's not go into how I had to simultaneously conquer fears about driving abroad and driving over many viaducts and bridges). She regularly travels to London using public transport and has started sharing her singing videos with her family and friends. She is a talented singer songwriter who is still finding her voice and her feet. She has a story. She is a survivor. She's the reason I am here today writing this book. I have had to face so many fears and so has she. She inspires me daily to step out of my comfort zone and live my best life. All my children do. The best of my life is on the other side of the fear fence, and unless I am prepared to get over that fence, my best life eludes me. The same is true for you.

So what are you afraid of? What is the fear that keeps you up at night or prevents you from living your best life? What is the thing that creates so much terror in your life?

The Effects of Fear On The Body and Mind

There are many effects on the mind and body, and when explored the negative impact of fear is significant.

Physical

- Breathing difficulties
- Tightness in the chest
- Shaking or trembling
- Faster or irregular heart rate
- Dizziness or light headedness
- Hot or cold flushes
- Perspiration
- Tummy pains and digestive stress

Mental/Emotional

- Panic attacks or overwhelming anxiety
- An awareness of feeling detached from self
- Desire to run or escape the situation that created the fear
- Feeling out of control
- Feeling of powerlessness
- Feeling faint or as if you may die

If we study the 'fight, flight or freeze' response to fear, we can see how it starts in our mind and follow the impact it physically has on our bodies. The information below was taken from research conducted on the effects of chronic fear on a person's health conducted by Mary D. Moller, an associate professor at Pacific Lutheran University School of Nursing and Director of Psychiatric Services at Northwest Centre for Integrated Health in the US. *

When there is a perceived threat, the body has three natural responses:

1. The first response is a reaction to danger. In the brain, the hypothalamic-pituitary-adrenal axis (HPA) and autonomic nervous system are activated. Then the primary stress hormones cortisol, adrenaline and non-adrenaline are released.

2. Stress hormones return to normal, but defences may be reduced.

3. Due to the prolonged stress levels, the body is less able to resist and may be left feeling exhausted or burned out.

Moller's research described various physical affects arising from reaction to chronic fear on the body. These can include migraine headaches, body aches and pains, breathing difficulties, fibromyalgia from muscle stress as well as many others. For me, I get tense muscle spasms from holding my body in a tight, frozen position. Ironically, writing about this, I feel tension in my shoulders and back as I relate back to the many fearful moments in my life.

Moller also talks about how there is a significant impact on the mind and emotional health caused by chronic fear. Negative thinking can create dissociation from self, extreme mood swings, unhappiness, anxiety, depression and being unable to connect to others on a loving level, and paranoia. Prolonged exposure to fear can also create a spiritual dissociation and can reduce the brain's capacity to effectively store and process information.

~~~~~~~~~~

I once had a boss who I was terrified of upsetting. She was pleasant enough as a person, but when she was under pressure or stressed, her lips would pinch together and her eyes sharpened like lasers. She would then adopt a spiteful, bitter voice spoken through gritted teeth. 'We need a meeting. Now!' she would spit out tensely and just above a whisper.

This was over twenty years ago, but I remember vividly the feeling in my stomach upon hearing those words. My blood would freeze to ice and my organs seem to melt into sludge. My tongue would glue itself to the roof of my mouth and my heart would pound in my chest. My limbs would leaden and my mind crumble. Thoughts would be racing and incoherent in my head.

When this woman adopted this bullying stance with me, my initial response was always to freeze. Then I would want to escape but couldn't. Fighting her was never an option. However, I have been attacked by a couple of men on two separate occasions as a teenager and my initial response was anger or 'fight'. On those two occasions, I displayed an instinctive 'fight' reaction to a fearful, dangerous threat to me.

With this bullying boss, I was in no position to ever argue my case and when she did speak to me this way, my stomach dropped in a downward flushing sensation and I always thought I would poo myself. I totally get it when people remark 'I was so scared, I almost crapped myself!' She was a bully and I allowed her to bully me because I hadn't learned tools to strengthen myself, believe in my voice or stand up to her. I take comfort in knowing she lost her job months after I left, but before then, I felt forced out of a great job by her irrational behaviour and the fear I allowed myself to be subjected to. If I had been stronger at the time, I would have remained in that position and inherited her Director role within a year.

I will never allow anyone to treat me that way again. However, bullying is something I have had to face my entire life, from various people who should have loved, nurtured and supported me: people who should have had my back unconditionally. Over the past few years, I have learned to stand up to bullies by strengthening my self-worth and thus giving myself a stronger internal voice that consequently resulted in making decisions best for me and my own personal wellbeing. I have learned the tools I am showing you and now live a freer, more self-aware and self-loving life. Though in hindsight, I wish I had learned these skills sooner, thus allowing me to release myself earlier from the grip of all those various bullying hands on my life. As the Dalai Lama said,

'Happiness is not something readymade. It comes from your actions.'

How many of you can relate to a childhood filled with fear, abuse, neglect, lack of love and nurture? That fear doesn't dissipate with growth and ageing if not dealt with. It simply gets hidden and then rears its ugly head when a situation, crisis or trauma triggers it back into our space. At some stage the fear has to be embraced, confronted in its gruesome face and challenged for what it is and let go of. Like a heavy, lead balloon attached to our bodies, it has to be released in our mind to diminish and disappear so we are lighter without this heavy burden.

I refer to the ancient philosophers, poets and theologians and mystic thinkers many times in the book, borrowing snippets of their wisdom as quotes to emphasise points. I particularly love the wisdom of the 13th Century Persian poet Rumi who wrote,

'Move, but don't move the way fear makes you move.'

It is time to let go of fear; there is no room for it in your life if you want to make changes, realise your dreams or move out of the place you are in right now. Although, as I have mentioned, fear is in the mind, it isn't easy to let that balloon go. Let's take another look at this word *fear* in an attempt to understand the impact it has on us.

When we are faced with a new situation, like a house or location move, a new job, a divorce or separation, a teenager leaving home to go to college or university, etc., we can experience feelings of loss, fear or anguish. Any of these situations could evoke a sense of foreboding, doom and fear of the unknown. We think of what we will lose rather that what we will gain. Change is not easy and we tend to focus on the things that could go wrong, hence we create obstacles to prevent us from taking the challenge or creating the change. We can find it hard to let go of the comforting known space to walk into what is not known. We use words like 'what if...?' in a negative way: What if I fail? What if I don't make new friends? What if it doesn't work out? What if I'm lonely?

Living in *what if* land isn't going to enhance your life one drop. Not unless it's flipped into a positive. For example, 'What if I go there and I meet my soul mate? Can you imagine how exciting that would be?' Sounds so much more hopeful than 'What if I move and am lonely and never meet anyone?'

To remove the negative 'what if' obstacles from your path, you will have to face the possibility that the outcome may be better than the present situation. Yes, that's right. It could be flipping amazing. How you react to an idea, concept or situation, is a choice, and the more you think about fear, the more fear builds up. Fear is a natural response to physical and emotional danger.

Fear is how our mind avoids pain, discomfort and change. It is there to protect us from a perceived threat. And if we look back to our primeval beginnings where humans lived in caves and faced danger daily, fear was a protective reaction against threat or death. This explains the existence of the 'fight or flight' responses. However, despite our survival chances improving and danger of imminent death significantly reduced in our day-to-day lives, this primitive reaction remains. We avoid challenge or situations that require us to step out of our comfort zone, for example, jumping out of an aeroplane with a parachute. I don't know about you, but my 'what ifs' kick in overtime on that one! Using a less extreme example, how many of us respond, either mentally or verbally, with a *what if* when offered a new opportunity?

Fear is an autonomic response. What does that mean? Well, Wikipedia describes it this way: *'The autonomic nervous system is a control system that acts largely unconsciously and regulates bodily functions such as heart rate, digestion, respiratory rate, pupil response, urination and sexual arousal.'*

So fear is a chain reaction that starts in the brain and ends up exposing itself as a physical reaction in our body. So let's re-read that. It starts in the brain; in our thoughts. If we can think of fearful things and our body reacts accordingly, then surely we could learn to flip that on its head and reverse the reaction?

Let's take a closer look at two types of fears: the fear of failure and the fear of success. Yes, you read the latter one correctly...the fear of things actually working out for us and thus becoming successful.

Let's explore the fear of failure first. Les Brown, the motivational speaker, author and invisible mentor to me (we just haven't met yet), speaks extensively about fears in his many speeches. I have referred to him at the end of this book and I hugely recommend listening to his teachings on audio or YouTube. It's my dream to meet him one day and give him the biggest hug for unknowingly guiding me through some very tough life times.

Brown says, *'Too many of us are not living our dreams because we are living our fears.'*

Fear is responsible for killing dreams, hopes, vision and ambition. Fear creates limitations in our mind. Living in fear means the *what ifs* are allowed to rule. Well, why not be different and override those fears to make room for your dreams and ambitions to thrive? We create obstacles in our lives and we become the obstacles. Ralph Waldo Emerson, the famous poet, lecturer and essayist of the mid-19th Century, wrote:

'Do the thing you fear and the death of fear is certain.'

We can lose our power to negative thinking and get trapped or paralysed by fear. Often when an opportunity arises, we can block it. There are many reasons we instinctively do this, including a worry that we don't deserve it, or that we will fail in the pursuit of the thing we desire. Ultimately, though, we have the power to dissolve those fears. It is simply a matter of choice. Children's author Rudyard Kipling spoke about the worst liars being our own fears. Is it time to let go of some of those fears that keep you trapped and imprisoned inside yourself? Is it time for you to listen to some fresh ideas to inspire yourself to let go and become a freer version of yourself?

'The ways of fools seem right to them, but the wise listen to advice.'

~ Proverbs 12:15

So, we have established what brought you here, what your mental state is and now we are delving deeper into your fears.

Guys, it's time to let them go. Success comes from falling down, getting back up and facing your fears time and time again. Fall, fail, get back up and carry on. Let's take a look at some of the ways to live a life free of some of those fears that may be holding you back or keeping you flat on the floor. Motivational speaker Les Brown says that if you fall, make sure you land on your back, because if you can *'look up, you can get up'*.

In the New Testament of the Bible, in Matthew 8 verse 26, it is written,

'Why are ye fearful, oh ye of little faith?'

The Fear of Failure

'When you fail at something, at least you are trying.'
~ Scottish Proverb

In the very lowest points of my life as a single parent, the fear of being a failure has been the most crushing. To not be able to sufficiently provide for my children has been my greatest fear. So imagine the impact that increasing debt and low income had, whilst attempting to rebuild my life after losing almost everything to trauma? I was flattened and in despair. When I say I have walked many of your paths, believe me, I wasn't lying.

There are two names given to the extreme phobia of an irrational fear of failing: kakorrhaphiophobia and atychiphobia. Before researching this, I didn't even realise that such phobias existed. Most people do not have an extreme phobia, but many people, including myself, have struggled with a fear of failure at some stage in their life.

The fear that we won't win, won't achieve, won't succeed in our goals, can keep us trapped and immobile and in 'stuckville' – an imaginary, yet seemingly real place for all the stuck peoples of this world. So what are we afraid of when we think of failing? What is the worst thing that could happen to us if our efforts to produce a winning outcome do not materialise?

When we don't succeed, we can feel an immense sense of shame and disappointment. We beat up on ourselves and perhaps stop trying altogether. It's not the act of failing that cripples, but the feeling of shame it induces. Nobody enjoys failure, yet it's a necessary part of our growth. So why is it a big deal to us that we feel so shameful when we fail at something, or we fail to retain what we achieved? As with the body and mind responses to extreme fear, there is a knock on reaction to feeling shameful.

Shame can have a negative effect on our self-perception. It can attack our self-esteem and cause us to react with a lower self-image because we feel we have failed. Shame causes us to worry about other people's perception of us and that other people's expectations of us will reduce. We believe that because of our failure, we have shrunk in capability in another person's eyes, or those of the wider community.

Shame can prohibit us from stepping out of our comfort zone or to try again. It is easier to give up on goals or intentions when the feelings of shame from failure overwhelm us. Shame is debilitating. It can stop us in our tracks and prevent us from going forward to achieve a goal or ambition.

Fear of failure can also lead to self-sabotage. We are often so fearful that we can delay or scupper projects, or even subconsciously plan to fail. Yes we actually can do that! I have been guilty of self-sabotage on a few occasions. One particular time cost me a relationship. I was so fearful that the guy would walk away because of my complicated family life, that this scenario literally plagued my mind. In the end, despite his reassurances to the contrary, that's exactly what happened. I believe I negatively **thought** this conclusion into being.

If this sounds a bit absurd to you, don't worry, it was a while before I could really grasp that we are capable of thinking something negative or positive into existence. We will discuss the power of the subconscious mind and conscious versus subconscious thinking further on in the book.

Before I leave this particular fear, let's remember those famous actors, writers, performers, artists, entrepreneurs and countless other well-known people who have spectacularly failed at some point in their lives, only to go on and achieve success in their field. Here are a few...

- JK Rowling, author of the Harry Potter series of books, was a desperate single mother on benefits, writing books in Edinburgh cafes. Her first book was rejected 12 times by publishers before finally being accepted. At her peak, her earnings were estimated around £1billion.

- Albert Einstein didn't speak until he was four and he was informed he was stupid. He was expelled from school for his rebellious nature and refused entrance to Zurich Polytechnic School. He became one of the most accomplished and renowned thinkers of all time. He once said *'Success is failure in progress.'*

- Bill Gates, the Microsoft founder and billionaire, failed in businesses before his success.

- Henry Ford failed in two businesses before his automotive success.

- Steve Jobs, the founder of Apple, was fired from his own company before going on to make huge successes at other ventures. He remarked that getting fired from Apple was the best thing that happened to him.

- Colonel Sanders, of Kentucky Fried Chicken (KFC) success, was rejected 1009 times before his now famous recipe was accepted. He had suffered numerous failed business ventures before aged 62 when he finally discovered success.

- Walt Disney was a multiple failure in business and suffered bankruptcy before he formed the Walt Disney Company.

- Oprah Winfrey got fired as a news reporter because she was too emotional. She then went on to create her highly successful Oprah daytime television show.

- Elvis Presley was informed by a radio host that he would be better off driving trucks than trying to make it in music. So pleased he didn't listen.

- Thomas Edison failed a spectacular 1,000 plus times before finally inventing a commercially viable electric lightbulb.

- Lord of the Flies by William Golding was rejected 20 times by publishers.

- Gone With the Wind by Margaret Mitchell was rejected 38 times.

- Steven Spielberg got rejected from the University of Southern California three times, and when he was finally at college, took 33 years to complete his college degree

You see, most people have failed at some point in their lives or at something. The difference is in whether you stay down or get back up again. Some successful people, as I have documented above, failed spectacularly and still managed to get on their feet and keep trying until success finally presented itself. Life throws up many obstacles on our journey and we can either see them as a roadblock or as an opportunity. I love this quote by the late Marilyn Monroe,

'Just because you fail once, doesn't mean you are going to fail at everything.'

Fear of Success

Can you believe that some people are afraid of success? Like the fear of failure, it even has its own phobia – achievemephobia. It's true! I looked it up!

People fear success for many reasons; from a worry of being a disappointment, to a terror of being seen, envied and judged. Often, when success happens quickly, for example, becoming a famous singer or part of a successful music band or even a big lottery winner, the person is in danger of overwhelm and can sink into a pool of anxiety. They may have worries about maintaining their success and the responsibility of letting others down if they fail. They can also worry about having too much money or material wealth and being seen as becoming showy or extravagant. Then there is the concern that they don't deserve success. Imposter syndrome can evolve from this fear. This is the feeling of being a fraud and no matter what successes are accomplished, the feeling pervades that it isn't deserved and we will soon be discovered to be a fraud. It's a horrible feeling and very common.

I can associate with this syndrome, as that's exactly how I felt when I first started out as a makeup artist. When friends or clients remarked positively on my work, I would knock them down or deny myself the feedback. Then one day, I realised that I had been doing this with all of my achievements throughout my entire life. To overcome it, I took a searching look at the reasons why I adopted this subconscious, self-sabotaging approach. It stemmed back from issues to do with my childhood and my own low self-esteem growing up and the feelings of being invisible within my family at a young age. It was time to let myself off the hook and appreciate what I achieved. Once you start loving yourself and being grateful for your gifts and talents, accepting your successes comes easier.

Fear of success is debilitating because it can prevent you from taking opportunities and risks that may lead to better and more positive outcomes. Fearing losing love, people, money, business and the material benefits of abundance can prevent the necessary steps to create those opportunities.

As already mentioned, it can also lead to self-sabotage. We often create our own glass ceilings. Take the example of a lottery winner. Statistics have proven that around 70% of lottery winners end up broke again. Why? Because of that old saying, *'A fool and his money are soon parted.'*

Most lottery winners do not possess a winner's mindset and they struggle with the overwhelming sudden change of circumstances in their lives. Overnight, they can have access to realising their dreams – the house, car, holidays of a lifetime, gadgets etc. etc. – all at the flick of their credit card. However, what most of these big lottery winners lack is the capacity to handle that financial gain. That's why they self-sabotage. They struggle to say no and give away much of their wealth to friends and family. They purchase without thought to the future and lavish money on things they want but don't need. Money then becomes less meaningful and often more complicated. Life was much easier when they dreamed of having money rather than actually having it. Their own limiting beliefs - a false belief based on past experiences - caused them to fear being successful and thus they subconsciously sabotaged their 'dream come true' financial success.

Becoming successful and wealthy is a process. Without going through that process, suddenly being handed a vast amount of money on a plate literally overnight, means that most people will not have the tools, wisdom and emotional development to be able to handle becoming an instant multi-millionaire.

It's all about the process. Becoming successful is a process. It's about having a goal, a vision, and progressing towards that goal, no matter what. Fearing success indicates that more personal development is required before success lands on your doorstep.

'There is no elevator to success, you have to take the stairs.'
~ Ancient Chinese Proverb

So now that you have acknowledged your fears, explored the word *fear* and the different types and examined its various causes and symptoms, it is time to look at ways of overcoming fear.

It is time to let go. It is time to learn how to be free so you can be free to be everything you were destined to be. In the words of Rumi,

'I want to sing like the birds, not worrying about who hears or what they think.'

Facing and Overcoming Fears

'The man who removes a mountain, begins by carrying away small stones.'
~ Ancient Chinese Proverb

We are the creator of our own lives. Simple. We get to choose how much fear plays a part in our lives. I referred earlier to actor Jim Carrey's speech. This is an excerpt of that speech in relation to his thoughts on fear:

'Fear is going to be a player in your life, but you get to decide how much. You can spend your whole life imagining ghosts, worrying about the pathway to the future, but all there will ever be is what's happening here and the decisions we make in this moment, which are based in either love or fear.'

It is worth remembering that it is not what you fear that holds you back, but the feeling of fear itself. What feelings does your particular fear evoke in you? Giving power to the fear exacerbates and intensifies the feelings evoked by the fear. For example, a friend of mine has a big awards ceremony in her professional field this weekend and she has been nominated for six awards. She has spent the past few days panicking about attending. The fears of both failure and success have attacked and plagued her mind with *what if* questions. This morning she awoke with a severe ear infection that sent her to the doctor. Such is the intense power of anxiety, worry and fear.

I gave her this advice: Imagine it's the end of the evening and you are standing in front of photographers with the one award you desire the most. You are smiling, laughing, ecstatic with joy, relief and happiness. The feelings inside you are incredible and you feel exhilarated.

'How does that image make you feel?' I asked her over the phone.

'Flipping amazing!' she replied. I could hear the excitement and joy in her voice.

'So do this,' I replied. 'When the panic and anxiety creep in to torture you, slot in this good feeling instead. Imagine you have already won the award and are smiling in front of the cameras thanking everyone.'

'Wow, even just hearing you say it aloud again makes me feel different.'

'And what does different feel like?' I asked her.

'Good. Different feels amazingly good.' I sensed her smiling. 'That really works. Thank you.'

She did indeed go on to win the one award she desired the most.

Fear is a choice; it is created in our minds by our imagination to protect us from the danger of a possible negative outcome. Let's emphasise that word *imagination*. How powerful is imagination, if it can create both a negative and a positive outcome based on what we *imagine* could be the outcome? Therefore why not create a new picture in your mind of the outcome you desire? Change the mind pictures, or what some thinkers and authors have called the 'mind movie.' These are the thoughts that play in our mind creating stories. If the mind movies played in your thoughts are full of fear, terror and anxiety, then the affect it can have on you is huge. Think back to my friend with the ear infection.

We have the ability to create new stories, new mind movies in our heads. For example, we can visualise a positive outcome to a situation or circumstance we are thinking of, instead of a negative outcome. I will explore visualisation and meditation later in this book, but for now try this experiment. Imagine this scenario:

You have a fear of flying and next week you have to take a flight for work. It's eating you up and the thought fills you with dread. Just thinking of getting to the airport and approaching that aeroplane physically causes you to perspire and your heart to pound in your chest. You may get a headache, or some other physical ailment. These are symptoms of fear caused by the response to the negative mind movie you have created in your mind.

What is the fear? Why are you afraid of flying? What is the worst thing that can happen? *"I crash!!!"* I hear a thousand voices cry. Yes that's true. That is the very worst possible outcome of being a passenger in a plane. It is also the worst outcome for being in a car, a train, a bus, a motorbike, a pushbike, a boat, a helicopter or any other moving transportation. Walking is dangerous, so is running, skiing, skating, hopping, skipping and jumping. Damn it, just stay in bed! Oh wait, what if the roof falls down whilst you are under your duvet? Jokes aside, life is full of risks every single day from waking to going to sleep, yet we still get up and do life.

Every day we take risks from possible external situations occurring to affect the safety of our lives. Yet there are internal factors kicking around in our bodies also responsible for fear, such as disease, illness, ailments, afflictions, physical conditions and extreme reactions to foods, animals and other things. Unless physically unable, we get out of bed each morning to face the world. We cannot live in debilitating fear, and the majority of us choose not to do so. Most of us wake up, have a morning routine, wash, eat, drink and leave the house.

So let us return to the example of the fear of flying and the fear of the aeroplane crashing. It does happen, of course, as do car crashes and falling down ditches and breaking legs on a country walk. However, the chances of it happening are very rare.

I took a look at the statistics. According to research, the likelihood of being in a plane crash is close to one in 11 million. The odds are higher to get struck by lightning or attacked by a shark. What may be comforting if you think those plane crash statistics are still high enough to be terrified, is that 95% of plane crash victims do survive.

So let's take this particular fear of flying and using the mind movie technique to create a more positive outcome to focus on. Close your eyes (read this paragraph first and then try the exercise). Breathe in deeply for a count of three. Breathe out for a count of three. Repeat three times. Let go of all thoughts that float into your mind: see those distracting thoughts as red balloons and watch in your mind as they float away. Empty your mind of everything and smile. You are feeling peaceful and content. Then imagine yourself on the aeroplane. You are sitting in the seat and talking to a stranger seated next you. You are smiling and you feel happy. The person asks why you are so happy. You tell her (it's a woman) that you haven't had a holiday for two years and you are so excited. You have packed your summer clothes and sandals and can't wait to hit that beach. You talk about the weather and the country you are flying to; it is beautiful, sunny and hot. The country you are in now is getting colder as winter encroaches and your nose is already pink and you are getting the sniffles. You have worked so hard to afford this holiday. You literally cannot wait to get on that beach. You tell her you are meeting a friend there whom you haven't seen for quite a while and you are looking forward to relaxing and to switching off. The thought of it makes you smile and you tell the woman how happy you are to be going on holiday.

Feel that smile. Feel that excitement. Imagine yourself getting off the plane on the other side, feeling the warm air on your cheeks and that joy of 'I'm here!' flooding through your veins. The relief of having finally arrived and the anticipation of the great times ahead; let it swell your heart with joy.

Open your eyes. How do you feel after doing this exercise? Are you smiling, relaxed, feeling the warmth of the holiday sun on your face? Does this evoke memories of past holidays and great times abroad? Wouldn't you rather feel these feelings than ones of *what if?*

If the answer is yes, then you have created a new mind movie as a technique for handling that particular fear. It can be used for all types of fear. By imagining a more positive outcome and experience the emotions attached to that imagined positive outcome, we can change the movie in our heads. Through using our imaginations to change the focus of our thoughts, we can change our response to a situation. This is so powerful. It allows you to step into that new picture you created in your mind and challenge the narrative in your head. By creating a new mind movie and re-conditioning your thought process, you can write a new ending for your fear.

What if this fear is a person? Maybe it's a sibling, a parent, a teacher, a boss, a colleague, a partner, spouse or simply a bully. This technique is highly effective in helping you manage the fear related to that person, because you can visually change the impact by changing their shape, size, colour and even anatomy.

Sound crazy? Try it. Think of someone who you know evokes in you a feeling of foreboding. Imagine them standing in front of you. Then change their appearance to a small, cute grey bunny rabbit with huge floppy, soft ears that lop down over its face. His eyes are so round and cute and his little nose twitches in expectation as he looks at you. He is so adorable, you want to pick him up and cuddle him.

Through the use of mind association, in your imagination, this bully has been reduced to a cute little bunny rabbit. Or what about imagining them as a small egg? There is very little to fear about a small, solid egg. By turning a bullying father into the image of a small egg on the ground, the fearful power he once may have held is taken away or dramatically reduced.

It's a powerful image, right? And it didn't take long to conjure up, or use up too much mental energy. The effect of this technique can be transforming. Next time that bully causes you to break out in a panic, try the egg or the bunny image and see if the panic diminishes. It may take some practise, but it is a powerful mind tool to help combat fear.

We have the power to change our lives through thoughts and actions, and we can use this power to conquer fears. We will explore the power of our thoughts and language in the next chapter.

'Life is an echo, what you send out, comes back. What you sow, you reap. What you give you get. What you see in others, exists in you. Remember life is an echo. It always gets back to you.'
~ Ancient Chinese Proverb

Jack Canfield, the author of the Chicken Soup for the Soul books, suggests this exercise in his 2018 video 'How to Overcome the Fears You Create'. First, write a list of the things you are afraid to do. The next step is to write down the fearful outcome and then change the negative outcome to a positive outcome. Here is an example.

Fear: Going to the Awards Ceremony

Negative Outcome:
I won't win anything and I will feel like a failure and let down

Positive Outcome:
I will win at least one award and my achievements will be recognised, my career will be progressed and I   will   feel amazing

By changing our perspective on a situation, we have the opportunity to change the outcome. In the above exercise, a negative, fear based outcome was changed to a positive, successful outcome, by changing the mental picture. It's so clever!

I loved this bit of wisdom I once found in a fortune cookie:

'Nothing is so much to be feared as fear.'

Fears are painful; we have explored that. Their impact on us can be huge: physically, mentally and emotionally. To overcome these fears is a real challenge. However, growth comes in working through the challenges. Truth. Nobody said it would be easy. Think of a child's growing pains. My son is a tall boy for his age and he often complains of his legs hurting. On occasion, the pains have been so unbearable that we visit the doctor. 'It's just growing pains' the doctor would confirm time and time again. Next thing you know, the little guy has grown a couple of inches. Growth is painful but necessary.

Suggested Steps on Overcoming Fears

1. Face your fear – confront the fear head on. By bringing it out into the open and acknowledging fear, it can be less terrifying. Sit through your fear; breathe through it and bring it out into the open.

2. Focus on the moment, the now, the present. Anxiety, after all, is worrying over a future event or circumstance.

3. Understand your fear. There is usually a reason for your fear. Once you acknowledge the source, the fear reduces in power. Go back to the source and understand the origin of the fear. Acknowledge that memory and confirm to yourself that you are letting go of that particular fear associated with that memory. Imagine it's a balloon and let it go.

4. Look at the evidence, educate yourself and gain a sense of proportion. For example, let's observe the fear of spiders. Stop a moment and look at that terrified spider trying to escape. Compare your size to it. It doesn't stand a chance against you and it probably isn't having a screaming, near heart attack fit like you are during your motionless stand-off with each other! Know your facts. What is it you are scared of? Spiders rarely bite or go into your mouth when you sleep and are not going to increase in size simply

because you caught it running across your living room floor! Be realistic and observe the facts.

5. The power of visualisation and creating mind stories/movies: Imagine a more positive outcome and remove the negative *what ifs* from your vocabulary. Stop catastrophizing. Change the mind story and visualise a perfect outcome.

6. Mental mapping – this is a person's point of view perception, or a perception of their own space. It is a visual mapping technique that provides brainstorming thoughts, techniques and strategies to move away from fear and into new areas of possibilities.

7. Share your fears and get them out into the open. Talking and sharing are positive tools for overcoming fears, particularly for extreme fears and phobias.

8. Make a plan. If your fear is of failure or success, for example, make a detailed plan of action to achieve your goal or goals. Thinking long term about achieving your goal may help resolve those immediate negative feelings of *what if?*

9. If your fear is public speaking, practise, practise and more practise, will help build confidence. Hearing your speech aloud can be helpful to correct intonation, pitch and gaining confidence in speaking those words. Try engaging friends or family to listen to the presentation and if you are brave, ask them for constructive criticism at the end.

10. Adopt a 'say yes' attitude. Saying yes to something may cause you to quake in your boots, but it could also allow the thrill of the challenge to lighten your day. Go for it! What have you got to lose by saying

yes? You may lose far more by turning down the opportunity due to your worries and fears.

11. Be kind to yourself and acknowledge that you want to overcome your fears, and this makes you brave and courageous. Affirm 'I am courageous in facing my fear'.

12. Use techniques such as meditation, E.F.T. (Emotional Freedom Techniques) hypnosis, NLP (Neuro-linguistic Programming), therapy, life coaching, yoga and low impact martial arts such as Chi Gong and Tai Chi. These are all alternative therapy techniques that can either be learned, taught or explored with a professional. I have used all of these to help me overcome my own fears, worries and anxieties.

13. Have gratitude. Giving thanks up and out (it doesn't have to be to anything specifically) is a great distraction technique when you feel fear. For example, if you are in fear of an awards ceremony, focus instead on feeling grateful for being nominated and invited to attend.

14. Write down your fears. Get them out of your head and down on paper.

15. Let go of the control. Release the hold that fear has on you by consciously letting it go.

16. Get motivational. Read self-help and motivational books to help you. Congratulations for reading this book!

17. Finally, ask yourself what's the worst thing that can happen? Flip the thought! Reverse the fear, see the positive and embrace the opportunity.

There are no doubt countless more techniques to overcome fear. Don't stop at my list – do some research of your own and you could find one that absolutely works for you! Finally, in the words of Rumi who has featured so much already in this book,

'Wake up! This world that you dream holds nothing to fear.'

Chapter Summary

1. Understand the shape you are in.
2. Recognise your fears.
3. Understand the effects of fear on your emotional, mental and physical wellbeing. Flight, flight or fear responses.
4. Face your fears.
5. Techniques and tools to overcome your fears.

Case Study 6: Anne - On Bullying

'I used to be crippled by fear on a daily basis. I looked like I had it all together but was 'tortured' by a feeling that something bad was going to happen. I would worry about the worst happenings to mundane things like not being a good enough mum.

I was a constant worrier until I started meditating and really looking into it.

When my dad died a lot of stuff came up to be cleared. He was a violent, aggressive man who beat me up weekly as a child. I was once left with broken ribs after one beating. It was only me who was targeted, as my two other sisters were 'good girls'. I left when I was sixteen and lived with a friend for a year, then joined the Navy. After that I went to Uni and was the first to graduate out of my family.

I was always a people pleaser for fear that a situation might turn out bad and then I would blame myself. The fear was instilled in me as a child. I learned to bury it with being successful, but it came up to the surface tenfold after my first child was born and again when my dad died. I feared and hated him for so long that I had no feelings for him except disgust for what he did. It only left when I learned to forgive what happened in my childhood and the fear began to leave.

I don't blame him. He just didn't know how to channel his own anger. I still have horrible fear arising, but I recognise it for what it is and I work through it. I think that's why I became a nurse, as I wanted to really help others, and in doing this I forgot about the painful childhood I had.

I let go of the shame and fear as I felt responsible, and I flood any situation with love and light.

Life is good and I survived that situation. I normally don't share this, but it was really powerful for me to let it out and let it go...even writing about it lets it go.'

~Anne, Nurse and Business Owner, Glasgow, Scotland.

Case Study 7: Emma – Fear of Failure

'It was over two years since I had last been on a date. When Eddie and I broke up, I was heartbroken. I didn't think I would ever be able to fall in love again. So one night, my friend Sarah set me up on a blind date with a colleague of hers from work. I said no for weeks, but she kept nagging me. I didn't think I was ready, to be honest, but she kept saying it would be good for me. This guy had also been left heartbroken by a break up. I can see what she was doing and looking back, I totally don't blame her. Two people she knew who were single and missing their exes; on paper, we probably seemed perfect for each other.

So after being asked constantly for weeks, on one drunken night out with her and the girls, I gave in and said yes. She messaged him immediately that night and he told her he'd check me out on social media and get back to her. Of course, I had already looked him up and he was pretty fit to be honest. He was dark and had a beard and a fit body, so he was just up my street.

Stupidly, I started to get excited. The next day, I messaged Sarah to see what he said. He hadn't responded yet. She assured me that it would be fine as she spoke to him about me and he said he was up for it.

Days went by and the good feeling turned to anxiousness. I felt so insecure waiting for Sarah to message me. I didn't feel I could hassle her again, so I left it and kept looking up his profile. Then I started to like some of his posts. He was quite a funny guy and some of his posts got me cracking. I think I even commented on a couple. I didn't see the harm in doing so, as we were going to be meeting anyway.

Then one afternoon, about a week after I had agreed to go on the blind date, Sarah messaged me. 'Sorry Em,' she started, 'but Greg doesn't want to meet up.' 'Why?' I asked, crestfallen.

'Truthfully?' she said. 'Yes!' I replied, thinking he got scared and had cold feet or something. There was a pause before she said, 'Have you been stalking him on Facebook?' My blood went ice cold and seemed to shrink away from my body. 'Course not!' I lied. 'Really? Cos he says you keep liking his stuff and leaving comments. Em...?'

Turns out he was thinking about whether he was ready to meet someone else and was about to agree to the date, when he kept seeing my name popping up on his posts. He blocked me in the end and told Sarah he thought I was a weirdo and there was no way he was dating a nutter after the break up with his girlfriend. She apparently put him through hell with her insecure jealousy.

I was mortified. Sarah and I have laughed about it since, but it was a long time before I dated anyone and she never suggested a blind date with anyone she knew again.'

~ *Emma, 27, Recruitment, London.*

Case Study 8: Palma – On Fear of Public Speaking

'The Fear of Life and Public Speaking

I was five when I started talking to the Universe! I sat on my window ledge outside of my bedroom window. I wanted to see, feel and experience everything! I set my intention.

I would watch the presenters on TV and copy them. I walked in my parents' room, and walked up and down mimicking their body language.

I went to drama college, loved it, and found I was a natural, but then I would lose my confidence. My dyslexia held me back. What if I could not read the auto cue? What if I pronounced words incorrectly? What if I was not good enough? I questioned myself and doubted myself. But my anxiety propelled me forward. It is my alchemy. My fear pushed me to be seen.

I was like a bow and arrow, pulling back then gliding fast forward. I would be so colourful and frantic. My drama teacher said 'Rein it in; that's the power!' This has taken me years to perfect.

Personal development, stepping out of my comfort zone and repetition are the only way to perfect any art form. But guess what? I love public speaking. However, I still get nervous and that's good. I'm a human being with emotions. I own them and express them consistently.

I use my nervous energy and breathe. I warm up my lips, mouth and voice. I take control, calm my mind. I visualise success, people applauding. Once on stage and my adrenaline calms down, I love it. It's trust for myself and for the audience. My mouth always dries up; that's the same feeling for excitement as it is for fear. So just take a sip of water, then continue. These are normal reactions to both fear and excitement. Turn the fear into excitement and say 'I am in control. I love this feeling'. Remember the previous time and look up and have gratitude.

I love comedy so I laugh a lot at myself too. I have the tools to succeed, plus I show my vulnerabilities with power! I am a powerful, real natural public speaker and my mission is to help others. That's the end in my mind, not my ego!

~ With love, Palma Palmer Esteem (so good they named me twice).

CHAPTER 4

TRAIT 3: **WATCH YOUR LANGUAGE**

'Your word is your wand. The words you speak create your own destiny.'
~ Florence Scovel Schinn

I love this quote. It's everything I now believe in. How we approach things very much depends upon our thought process. For example, today it is pouring outside and yet I choose to hold sunshine in my heart. How I did this was by using happy memories to make me smile. This morning on the school run, I brought up fun memories for the children, using the words, 'Do you remember when...?' instead of discussing the torrential rain pounding our car, or the deep puddles we were forced to drive through, or the inconvenience of backing up the car for five minutes to let other cars pass on the winding country lane on the back route to school. All other roads were crammed with rush hour traffic enhanced by the torrential downpour.

Instead we laughed as we recalled past moments. Kids love the 'Do you remember when...?' happy stories. I hope the kids went to school today with sunshine in their souls, rather than feeling blue because of the rain and the delays and the traffic and how their mother allowed those things to negatively affect her and as a result, them.

I never used to be like that. In the midst of the change, my unhappy moments during the dying light of my marriage and the heartbreak of the trauma years, I was wound up like a cotton reel. I was so tense that my shoulders ached and my back was constantly in pain. At one point, I had intense jaw pain from night grinding and I was forced to purchase an expensive, custom-made mouth guard just to protect my teeth overnight and relieve the tension in my jaw.

Those symptoms of worry, stress, anxiety and downright feeling unhappy have disappeared. My body still informs me when I need to let stuff go, like recently holding onto money worries. That resulted in putting out a rib from a chest infection and a continuous trapped nerve that moved from one side of my neck to the other. It took five osteopathy treatments for me to realise I couldn't hold onto that worry any longer. Instead, I turned to gratitude – for the things I do have rather than the stuff I don't. The feeling of lack has been a real killer for me. The realisation that I am not getting to my destination any quicker if I twist my insides into worry knots was quite an eye opener. That was the heaviest and hardest lead balloon to get rid of and I've only just let it go. I saw a quote recently that went something like this:

'Be grateful for what you have instead of focusing on what is missing.'
~ Author Unknown

Two years ago before I made a conscious decision to change my mindset and my approach to life, I was guilty of focusing on my lacks rather than what I had or what my achievements were. In fact, when I had a big birthday looming, I didn't want to celebrate the day. I was so disappointed to not have achieved what I thought I would have by that age that I didn't feel the desire to celebrate. I was so focused on what was missing in my life, that I couldn't see what I already had accomplished. It was two days after my birthday that the realisation hit me. So what if I didn't have those things? So what if I was still single? So what if I still rented my home and did not yet live in the impressive, white mansion I promised myself a year or so earlier? These things are unimportant in the grand scheme of life. It was a huge turning point for the way I perceived things. In fact, it was a wakeup call to 'get a grip'!

I still have to work on my mindset every day. It's an on-going process, but because of the tools in my bag and the techniques I have learned, the process gets easier and I am able to flip the negative thinking to a positive one quicker than before. This morning, for example, I could feel panic creeping in over money. However, because of the tools I have acquired and the knowledge that worry and anxiety and negative thinking are not beneficial to any situation, I could let it go within minutes. I was so proud of myself.

I used to beat myself up all the time. Not physically, of course, though in my most dire moments, I have slapped my face; such was my self-loathing reaction caused by the situations and circumstances I found myself in. It's so easy to take the negative, self-admonishing walk when life throws lemons at us.

Beating ourselves up can lead us into all sorts of problems. Apart from constantly feeling unhappy and seeing the world through a dark and troubled lens, we leave ourselves open to the impact on our health. Ailments, illness and disease can start to impact our wellbeing. Our mental health is threatened and our unhappiness can drive us towards anaesthetising our pain and numbing our emotions with substances and unhealthy coping mechanisms.

There are many ways we anaesthetise our pain and avoid confronting our emotions and as I mentioned earlier, I am no doctor or expert. Some are subtle, like using humour or sarcasm, to varying distraction techniques such as not listening, criticism, deliberate silence, preoccupation, procrastination, being overly busy, negative thinking, judging, anger and prejudices. Then of course there are the addictions that create a distraction to prevent us from facing up to whatever pain or unhappiness is going on inside us. These aren't just the usual suspects like drugs, alcohol and food, but also starvation, overworking, over exercising and food control. The list is much bigger, but you get the picture.

So many of us are so unhappy or unwilling to confront our pain, that we choose to hide behind a destructive behaviour or addiction, whether consciously or unconsciously. This is dangerous territory and the reason why learning techniques to flip those negative, destructive emotions and thoughts to more positive and healthy ones are crucial for our physical, emotional and mental wellbeing.

The Impact of Negative Self Talk

'The man who says he can and the man who says he can't are both correct.'
~ Confucius, Ancient Chinese Philosopher and Politician

Self-talk is the endless stream of unspoken thoughts that we entertain daily in our heads. We all do it; beat ourselves up on a regular basis with our own, negative self-talk. If you don't think you are guilty of this, when was the last time you spoke the words, 'I can't...' 'I'm not...' 'Silly me', or 'I'm so stupid!'?

Research conducted by Dr Masara Emoto, a Japanese author and pseudoscientist, discovered through various experiments that the molecular structure in water can be physically altered through the words and thoughts of the human consciousness. He did this through Magnetic Resonance Analysis Technology and photography.

His research claimed that after good, kind and encouraging words were spoken into water, beautiful crystals formed. He also conducted research on how sound can have an impact on the crystalline effects of water. For example, classical music produced beautiful crystalline patterns.

Alternatively, when negative, harsh or critical words were spoken into the water, or the sound was harsh, like heavy metal music for example, less attractive or ugly crystalline patterns were formed.

He backed up his research by displaying various crystals in petri dishes, with different molecular structures depending on the words spoken to it. The results indicated that if words and thoughts and intentions can influence water in such a way, then what affect does it have on human beings whose structure is 60% water?

Thus the impact of words, thoughts and intentions on us is significant. Whether our words and thoughts are positive or negative, we are impacted. So to not allow ourselves to be impacted negatively, we should speak only positive, kind and helpful words into ourselves and to others.

Whether you believe that there is validity to the experiments Emoto conducted or not, it's an interesting example of the impact language can have on our emotional wellbeing.

Personally, I love how beautiful, positive words and music affected the water droplets to create stunning crystal formations. It is worth looking up the experiments to see the crystalline formation research results.

~~~~~~~~~~~

The majority of us unconsciously spurt out self-admonishing words on a daily basis. We are constantly bombarding ourselves with reminders of our weaknesses, and our failures. As a result, we can get into a habit of thinking this is the normal way to speak to ourselves. At what stage did this become acceptable? At what point in your life was it okay to call yourself fat, stupid, ugly, useless, incapable, pathetic etc.? These are just some of the words I was guilty of repeating to myself on a regular basis.

I would never speak to friends, colleagues or a family member like this, so why did I think it was acceptable to speak to myself in such a condemning, condescending and derogatory manner?

Your words are powerful. Whether negative or positive, the words you speak or even think have a huge impact. Even the words in your head affect you.

You inner critic debilitates you. It limits you and can stop you living the life you really want. It steals your inner peace of mind and puts stress on your emotional wellbeing. The inner critic is self-destructive, and each time you speak to yourself in a nasty, critical tone, you are dropping a hate bomb inside you that has an imploding effect on the health of your emotional and physical wellbeing.

Imagine this scenario if you can:

You are walking down the street, feeling fairly happy, with a slight bounce in your step. You cross the road to the other side of the street and are confronted with your image reflecting back at you in the shop window ahead. It's not a flattering image as the window is slightly distorted. You don't see that, you just see the unflattering image reflecting back at you.

'Urghh!' remarks the voice inside your head. Your body hears that sound and takes the remark deep inside. Your smile dissipates from your face and you feel your lips pursing and your eyes lower to avoid the sight before you, or to scrutinise all your faults. Your shoulders slump a little; the spring in your step has gone and you feel like hiding. Someone accidentally bumps into you but doesn't apologise. You are feeling put upon and scowl. From that point on, everything seems to go wrong. The supermarket doesn't have your favourite item, you chose the wrong queue at the checkout, you overrun your parking ticket, everyone seems miserable and you just can't wait to get back to the sanctum of home or work.

Had days like that? Whilst I am not suggesting all those following mishaps would not have happened if your response to viewing your image in the shop window was less self-critical, the likelihood is that your inner, critical dialogue made the day less enjoyable. Hypothetically, the negative affect of saying 'Urggh!" on seeing your reflection may have impacted your response to the person bumping into you and your perception of the sequence of events that seemed to conspire against you.

Be kind to yourself. Treat YOU as you would like others to treat you. After all, you are your best friend and know YOU better than anyone else could. Begin by watching your words and your thoughts. Make a mental note, or scribe in a notepad, or some other place you can reference, the amount of times you use negative language on yourself. Look out for the following words or phrases:

I can't
I won't
I'm not
I haven't
I shouldn't
I couldn't
I'm so stupid
I'm so silly
Silly me
You're so stupid (your name)
I'm not good enough
I'm not worth it
I'm useless
There's no use

I'll never

It will be an interesting exercise, believe me.

There are actually four types of negative self-talk that we engage in regularly. See if you can relate to any of these listed below.

1. **Filtering** – we look at a situation and glean only the negative aspects from it and ignore or get rid of the positive aspects.

2. **Personalising** – blaming yourself when something goes wrong

3. **Catastrophizing** – looking at the worst possible outcome or anticipating the worst to happen

4. **Polarising** – only seeing the good or the bad and not an in-between, middle ground. For example – you have been on a diet for seven days. You have lost two kilos and feel amazing. Then one day you break that diet with a slice of birthday cake. You feel like a failure and verbally beat yourself up.

I've been guilty of all of these because I used to be a perfectionist, a control freak in an out of control environment. In fact, a few out of control environments. It was pretty ugly in my head at times. Thankfully, I have learnt to let go of control and expecting perfection from myself. I have immense goals, but now celebrate the small wins as well as aim for lassoing the moon.

The Impact of Negative Self-Talk on Our Mind and Bodies

When our inner critic is talking, things happen to our body and our emotional wellbeing. Our self-esteem takes a battering and our confidence is affected. We go into a low vibration mode and our energy levels deplete. Talking or thinking negative to oneself has no benefits to our emotional wellbeing. In fact, the very opposite is true.

Being self-critical, talking negatively to oneself, or thinking bad self-thoughts, limits our ability to believe in ourselves. We move into a victim mentality and miss or ignore opportunities and the chance to make more positive, beneficial changes to our life. We feel more stressed and may suffer from anxiety or depressed thoughts. We may be prone to distraction, procrastination, inertia and feelings of helplessness. We often feel 'stuck.'

Saying phrases such as 'I can't' or 'I'm not' limits our thinking and can prevent us from pursuing our goals or making decisions that are positive steps towards those goals. The more we repeat those negative, self-critical words to ourselves, the worse we feel.

For example, school children learn spelling words on a repetition basis as well as the times tables. They are taught to repeat these over and over until they stick in their memory, to be pulled out as and when required throughout their lives. The same then is true of the negative words and phrases we bombard ourselves with. They go deep into our subconscious and we believe these words to be the truth. Repetition is incredibly powerful on our memories. If we change those words to positive ones, the impact could be life changing.

After all, our subconscious mind believes what it is told, whether what we are telling it is the truth or not.

Often when we strive for perfection and don't hit the bar, the disappointment can be devastating. We may crumble or give up. Depression and anxiety may follow and then physical symptoms may develop as a result. The pressure we put on ourselves to achieve a goal, only to then fail, can often result in a barrage of self abusive chatter that may inhibit us from trying again.

Finally, others tire of us when we are constantly berating ourselves or repeatedly putting ourselves down. It's actually exhausting listening to someone who constantly criticises themselves. They can become tiresome to be around. And nobody wants to be around a bore given a choice.

If none of this is going to change your mind, let me take you down memory lane. Imagine a child (it could be you) at home or in a classroom environment. It has to be a space that resonates with you. Someone, a teacher or parent, calls them stupid. It sticks. Their friends start to call them stupid. A sibling might call them stupid at some point. They grow up thinking they are stupid. Their experience points to it; they have the evidence of the spoken word to corroborate that imposed judgement. The word was swallowed up and absorbed by their subconscious mind. 'I am stupid' they say often to themselves.

As they grow and mature, the word carries deeper meaning and has a greater impact on their choices. They don't enter competitions, or try hard at homework or coursework, because their self-perception is that they are indeed, stupid, so they will fail. As if by a self-fulfilling prophesy, they then go on to fail and so that term they adopted subconsciously as a label for themselves becomes their truth. Each time they fail at something, they declare that it's because they are stupid. The cycle continues, until at some stage they make the decision to challenge that label and affirm that they are not stupid after all.

The words we speak to ourselves are a choice. How we think and what we say to ourselves, is a choice.

If you are guilty of negative self-talk and negative thinking, then make a conscious decision to stop right now. You flipping have my permission! Here are some tips on how to do that.

Changing Your Inner Dialogue

'Your life is what your thoughts make of it.'

~ Confucius, Ancient Chinese Philosopher and Politician

So how do you get out of this self-destructive habit? After all, it is a habit, since we were not born spluttering out self-harming and critical words to ourselves!

Firstly, recognise that this is an adopted behaviour or a habit. As with most habits, it can take a while to break, and since this is a learned or repetitive behaviour, it's going to take a process of effort and re-structuring of your language and thought patterns. Here are some helpful tips to break away from those destructive patterns you may have adopted.

1. Take notice of your inner critic. What is your inner dialogue? How do you speak to yourself on a daily basis or when things go wrong? What is your verbal or thought reaction to stress or disappointment? Catch yourself in the moment or mid-sentence. You

have permission to say 'Shut up!' or 'Be quiet!' to yourself when the negative words or thoughts come into your mind or out of your mouth. Shut the critic up. In fact, say that as a mantra when you're being nasty to yourself: **'Shut the critic up!'**

2. Negative thoughts can be changed to positive thoughts. It's a choice. Train your mind to listen to your self-talk. Your mind will believe what you tell it, so why be mean when you really don't need to? Change your inner talk to something kinder.

3. Change your words to reduce their impact on you. For example, instead of saying or thinking 'I can't', say **'Yes I can.'** Shout it from the rooftops if need be.

4. Why not challenge your inner critic, or even give it a nickname? I call mine Blagpuss, a take on that lazy, saggy old cat from the children's television series of the 1970s. I think of my inner critic as a moaning, grumpy old cat having a go at me. Coming up with a name for your inner critic can be fun and very liberating.

5. Would you speak to a friend, family member or colleague like this? Give yourself more respect. Remember that you are showing others the way to treat you, so take more consideration of your own thoughts and feelings. Talking to yourself like you would someone you like, admire or love, can shift your negative self-talk to a more positive and loving one. Or at least cause you to be kinder to yourself!

6. Change your focus. Look at the features or characteristics you admire about yourself. Focus on those instead. Use the list below to write down the things you love or like about you.

7. Acknowledge the feeling; shame, guilt, feelings of helplessness or worthlessness are signs of the inner critic at work. When these feelings arise, take a moment to acknowledge them and stop them in their tracks by affirming phrases like **'You are doing great'**, **'You've got this'** or even **'You rock girl!"**

8. Grow a stronger, inner voice to challenge that inner critic. It will take practise, but since you were not born with an inner critic and grew it to the stage it's at now, you can grow a stronger ally to stand up against the detrimental damage this negative inner dialogue has on you. Fight back. How do you do this? By stating the great things about you. Challenge the bad with the good. Good always wins in the end (I refuse to believe otherwise).

9. Ask yourself this question when you find your inner dialogue spiralling down this critical route: **'IS IT TRUE?'** It invariably isn't. Challenge the inner critic by offering an alternative to the negative thought or statement. For example, if your inner voice says 'You're stupid', how about saying 'I may not think I'm perfect, but I love when I get things right. It makes me feel so happy. It's ok not to be perfect.'

10. It will take time to change these negative habits, as it's taken years to adopt and keep them. Be kind to yourself even in challenging the inner critic. Be patient, gentle and gracious. Baby steps. There are no failures, just lessons and steps in the right direction.

Let the final words on this go to Helen Keller, the American author who was the first deaf and blind person to earn a Bachelor of Arts at the turn of the twentieth century. She died in 1968 at the age of eighty-eight and was probably the most famous disabled person of her time. She wrote extensively about her life, whilst also becoming an activist for the disabled. She did not allow her physical disabilities to prevent her from achieving what she so remarkably did. She wrote,

'Keep your face to the sunshine and you cannot see a shadow.'

EXERCISE 5: WHAT I LOVE ABOUT ME LIST

Write at least ten things here that you like, love or admire about you. Be honest, frank and appreciative of all the things that are great about you. Above all, do not be self-depreciative or self-judgmental. This is your personal 'loving you' list. BE KIND to YOU, be honest and go for it!

The Power of the Spoken Word

So we have just looked at the impact that negative thinking and negative self-talk can have on our physical and mental wellbeing, but what about the positive impact on us from positive words and thoughts?

Words have power.

They have the ability to change lives, the ability to change our lives. How we communicate with ourselves and others is vital for an individual's healthy wellbeing. When you change your language to become more positive based, your world changes. People perceive you differently. Your energy and aura is far more attractive to others. In fact, you become more attractive. This is also true on a business level, since people respond more positively to positive messages.

There are so many reasons why changing the way we speak and think can have such a positive effect on our lives and on the lives of others around us. A significant percentage of our happiness can depend on our outlook on life. Whilst researching for this book, I saw this quote taken from a New York train:

'Your outlook on life is a direct reflection of how much you like yourself.'

By changing the conversations we have in our head and in our spoken words, we can change how we view ourselves and our perception of the world and in turn, how the world perceives us. How powerful is it to know that our words can have such a magnificent impact? Think back to some of the greatest speeches you have ever heard – Martin Luther King, Oprah Winfrey, JK Rowling, Malcolm X. These speeches inspired millions. They were positive words of hope and inspiration and desire for a better now and future. Their words also inspired inner change, as well as a desire for outer world change.

~~~~~~~~~~

Consider then, the power of your own words. Are they predominantly negative and self-criticising or uplifting and empowering? How you communicate with yourself and with the world is everything.

Today as I write this, I am brought to my own knees with this knowledge. I have been particularly low and down on myself the past thirty-six hours or so. I put working on this book aside as I knew I was struggling. Then I started writing up the notes from my research today and realised that the reason I'm low is because of the words I have been speaking to myself. They weren't unkind, but filled with doubt and feelings of lack and worry. 'I'm not, can't, haven't, aren't...' words like this have been spewing from my mouth, because I am running from doing the work. For whatever reason, we sometimes take a sick pleasure from acting out in the victim mentality.

I have many goals, dreams and desires for my life and I do more work on realising those than the majority around me, yet still I sometimes struggle with doubt and a feeling of lack. There are many times I have to use the tools I have in my bag to reel myself back to a good feeling.

This sense of lack is a killer for positive thinking. In our heads we see what we don't have, especially if we look around and compare ourselves to others. I am as guilty of this as anyone else, but I trust in the process. When I have low, negative self-talk days, I can gather myself back up to a happier, more self-rewarding place of hope and positivity.

So how do I do this? I watch my language. I catch myself in the act. I do all or a selection of the things I mentioned above to return to a happier state of being. It's a learned process, it takes time, and it works. One of these tools in my bag is to listen to those who have walked my chosen path before me. I pick up a book or switch on an Audible or YouTube video by authors, motivational or inspirational speakers and spiritual thinkers, like Dr Wayne Dyer. I cannot highly recommend enough to listen to their voices when the one inside your head feels more like an enemy than a friend.

I also have some fun with myself. Since I am single and edging middle aged, despite looking and feeling many years younger, I am prone to criticising my physical appearance (madness if you met me). So to combat these feelings of lack and not being *something* enough when I pass the mirror in my underwear, I wink at myself and say 'hey there sexy butt!' It's so ridiculous that I burst out laughing. I try not to take myself too seriously and that phrase really helps put my negative, self-berating thoughts back in the cardboard box they crawled out of! Try this tactic; I dare you. It's so hard to do at first, but when you get into the habit, you can't help but smile or laugh. An immediate mood turnaround!

The main reason for writing this book is to share what I have learned on my journey to help others to get their lives to a better place. Through the various challenges and difficult life experiences and the self-development work I have progressed through, my wish is to offer hope and inspiration to those countless women and men who are struggling or feeling stuck in their lives.

When we beat up on ourselves and lose our way, it's important to remind ourselves how far we have come and focus on gratitude rather than lack. We will look at gratitude in the next section of this chapter. When you can be happy in the place you are in now, then where you want to go begins to feel a whole load more exciting.

So if you want to move from the place you are in now and towards a better place, start with changing your language and refuse to beat yourself up any longer with negative, disempowering self-talk.

Remember that I have been in some very dark spaces and walked some pretty scary paths on my journey so far. I keep this ancient Chinese proverb near my desk, to remind me where I've come from and where I am going and why it's important for me to help others get out of that wretched stuck place they may be in:

'Only he that has travelled the road knows where the holes are deep.'

~ Ancient Chinese Proverb

Shifting Perspective

'We are what we repeatedly do. Excellence then, is not an act, but a habit.'

~ Aristotle

So how do we do this? How do we change the habit of how we speak to ourselves and to others? Firstly, take one step at a time. Negative self-talk is a learned habit and it takes a few weeks to break a habit that has possibly taken a lifetime to build up. Start small. Start by being more kind to yourself. Now that's a simple step, but if you are very down on yourself reading this, then it's also a gargantuan challenge.

Try this as a first step:

Imagine that you are someone you love or care about. It can even be a pet. It has to be someone you really care about and wouldn't want to hurt. Now, whenever you say or think something nasty to or about yourself, imagine you are saying it to them. See their reaction. Take in their reaction. How does your face look when you are spitting out this negative self-talk? Do you look loving, happy and at peace? No. You'll probably be wearing a sneer, a frown or a grimace. We aren't pretty when we are using negative self-dialogue.

Now try looking in the mirror and saying something kind and encouraging to the person looking back. Yes you. Go on; say something empowering. Try 'sexy butt'. Did you laugh or smile? It's hard to be mean-looking when you use positive words. Find the joy instead of the sadness, disappointment or self-hatred. I never said this was easy, but if you want to get up off that floor, out of that closet or back onto a winning path, then a perspective shift has to take place. And you might as well start right here, right now.

Go on, look in the mirror, do a little dance or wiggle and declare 'Sexy Butt!' as loud as you can. Wish I was there is all I can say. I would so love to see the transformation in your faces!

Shifting your language can shift your perspective on your life and your surroundings. You may start to see life in a different, fresher light. Throw some positive words into your daily life and see what happens. Use terms such as 'I am amazing', 'I rock!' or 'I am loved, lovely and loving'. I used this latter one almost every day to help me get through the trauma situation that almost broke me. I was so busy with self-loathing and disappointment, that I had a dark view of my life and the world around me. What helped the most was the line I forced myself to repeat over and over: 'I am loved, lovely and loving'. It affirmed my place as a mother, friend and decent human being. I needed to hear those words. They were incredibly powerful and affirming for me at that particular time; a time when I felt like a failure as a mother and a woman.

Words have energy and carry power. They can be used positively to uplift, inspire and encourage, or negatively to destroy and discourage. Using positive words can increase our perseverance and the way we approach tasks and situations.

The brain reacts quicker with positive words and allows us to be more proactive, attentive and creative. Using positive words can also have a physical impact on us as well as an improvement in mental wellbeing. The use of positive words and thoughts can actually strengthen areas in our frontal lobes and promote the brain's cognitive functioning.

Through the regular implementation of positive words

and thoughts, we can stimulate areas in the frontal lobe of the brain that can trigger a chain reaction in us, which in turn can stimulate positive action. Thus, if we have a goal or vision in mind, positive affirmations, words and thoughts can stimulate our brain into creating action steps towards achieving that goal. In fact, it has been written that success is indeed taking positive steps towards a goal or vision.

'If you correct your mind, the rest of your life will fall into place.'
~ Ancient Chinese Proverb

Ultimately, what all this means is that using positive words makes you feel happier. By flipping your words and thoughts to a more positive outlook, you actually feel lighter and more joyful. That in turn can change and improve your perception on life. This can also make you kick into action achieving a goal or goals. As with the example I used earlier of seeing your reflection in the shop window negatively and thus affecting your mood, using positive self-talk can actually infect the world around you positively, too.

Try this: Smile at someone when you are out today (or tomorrow if you are reading this in bed at night). A smile, like a yawn, is infectious. Invariably, most people will smile back. When you are driving, give way in the car. If you watch the car in front that you gave way to, they will often pay it forward with another car or pedestrian waiting to cross the road. When you feel good inside, you reflect it on the outside. This in turn inspires others to feel good also. How we think, talk and act, has a direct correlation on how we perceive the world, good or bad.

But let's face it, life can sometimes be a real shit. These are the really challenging times when no amount of self-help books is going to recover us from devastating news, a relationship breakdown, a loss of job, a serious illness diagnosis, or some other awful setback in our lives. That's why you picked up this book: because sometimes life sucks. I've been there and I know that painful place. I am writing this book not because I am a condescending know it all who has never experienced life's crappy times, but because I have. During the worst period of my life, I lay on my belly not knowing how to get up and when I did, I didn't know where to go afterwards. I begged God for help to set me straight again, and even when that that prayer was answered, I was so stuck I couldn't see the way out.

The tools I am offering are ones I used to get me to this place where I am today. They were tools given to me. If you take one golden nugget from all of the words I have written and it helps you move one millimetre forward, then it was worth it. As long as we move forward every day and not fall back and stay there, we are winning. Just keep moving and try not to go backwards.

I saw a quote recently from an unknown author that very much resonated with me: '*Look for something positive in each day, even if some days you have to look a little harder*'.

Before we move onto the power of gratitude, here are some suggestions on how to flip the negative to positive through words and thoughts. I have listed some common negative phrases below and some alternative positive ones to illustrate how we have the power to train our mind to change our words and thus positively influence and improve our perception of the world around us.

Negative	Positive
I'm really struggling I can't do it	This is challenging, but I will try
It's too hard for me	I'll have a go
I'm a failure	I'm a work in progress
I'm no good at that	I'm going to try my best
This is impossible	This is possible if I put my mind to it
It'll never happen for me	I believe I will achieve my goal/s

The Power of Gratitude

'Wear gratitude like a cloak and it will feed every corner of your life.'

~ Rumi

Why is having 'an attitude of gratitude' so important? The answer, quite simply, is because it makes us happier and is beneficial to our health and wellbeing. When a person is giving thanks and being appreciative, it is very difficult, if not impossible, to feel sad, depressed or low. Being grateful actually lifts our vibration. Even when our lives feel dark, trapped or lost, being in a state of gratitude can lift us up and help us up into a lighter sense of being.

When we acknowledge what is good and working in our lives, it edges out that feeling of lack and comparison. And when we really *feel* that gratitude for that person or thing, we feel it deep in our hearts. That heart vibration then shines out to uplift us and vibrate out to those around us. We actually become more pleasant to be around when we practise regular gratitude.

If this is a new concept to you, or one you have not yet practised, or deliberately avoided because of religious connotations, try a simple uplift of gratitude first. Simply say **'thank you'**. It doesn't have to necessarily be to anyone or to anywhere. The sound of those words coming from your own mouth is both liberating and empowering. Yes, empowering. Why? Because no doubt the journey you have been on that brought you to this place has been a wild and challenging one. Even if you have not experienced loss, pain, grief, heartache or a feeling of being lost, you may be feeling disempowered by the circumstances of your life.

There are twelve spiritual laws of the Universe, and one of them is The Law of Gratitude.

'The law of gratitude is the natural principle that action and reaction are always equal and in opposite directions.'

~ Wallace D Wattles, Author

Saying the words *thank you*, is a powerful healing tool for the negative state that you may be feeling. These two words can have a profoundly powerful impact on our daily outlook on life. Being grateful and expressing gratitude can improve physical health and wellbeing, as well as mental health and wellbeing.

Sounds incredible, right? That expressing two simple words directly to someone or indirectly to a Creator, Infinite Being, Universe, or to no one in particular, depending on your belief system, can have a direct correlation with your own wellbeing? Let's take a look at some of the benefits of practicing gratitude.

Attitude of Gratitude – The Health Benefits

- Better heart health
- Less stress
- Reduces anxiety and depression
- Helps fight disease and illness
- Raises energy and vitality levels
- Makes us happier
- Reduces negative thoughts
- Increases self-esteem and self confidence
- Boosts creativity
- Better sleep
- Reduces aches and pains
- Reduces feelings of anger, frustration, lack and resentment

- Encourages empathy
- Fosters resilience

Sounds pretty amazing doesn't it, to receive all these benefits from expressing two little words...*thank you*? But what if you are so low, so broken and unable to see one ounce of positivity in your life? If saying those words may seem utterly ridiculous to you, what should you do? You say them anyway. You say them for the rain, the sun, the warmth, the cool air, your bed, your waking up, your sleep, your health, your wealth, the food in your cupboards, in your fridge and the money you can still get out of your bank account.

Give thanks for your children, your friends, your family, your home, your car, your social environment and even your job. The list is endless. Seriously, just from two small words, spoken aloud or in your head, your life can improve in moments. And it's free! No sign ups, no expensive or time-consuming courses, no commitment; just a simple expression of gratitude.

Show appreciation for even the smallest of things. Find gratitude in the lessons and the difficulties and the challenges that those lessons offer. Believe it or not, it's in the sore times that we grow. Yes, those horrid moments that crush us and threaten to throw us as bait to the wolves; these are the times when we develop and grow the most as human beings. If you are scoffing right now and wanting to throw this book at the wall in anger and frustration, or me to those darn hypothetical wolves, I get it. I was there too. I couldn't bear to hear that the pain that I and my loved ones were going through was a necessary step towards becoming a better me.

'Arrghhh!' I would scream in frustration at those words. I was in such denial that a daily portion of gratitude into the ether was going to help me one iota. It took me a while to get my head around it, but once I started to practise the art of gratitude, then my life did start to improve.

I love this Dr Suess poem. I think it pretty much says it all about gratitude:

'When you think things are bad,

When you feel sour and blue,

When you start to get mad...

You should do what I do...

Just tell yourself, Duckie,

You're really quite lucky!

Some people are much more...

Oh, ever so much more...

Oh, muchly, much-much more

Unlucky than you!'

Being grateful despite your situation, disposition or circumstances, is not an easy choice at first, but start small. This is my daily gratitude routine that is now an integral part of my daily life.

On waking, I offer immediate gratitude for five to ten things. It's the first thing I do after turning off the alarm clock. Usually I offer thanks for waking up, then for my three children, for our home, for my car, my health, for food in the fridge and cupboard and for money in the bank.

Before I go to bed I repeat the process or if I am too exhausted to think, I will simply say *thank you*. Throughout the day, if I see the number eleven, I recite thank you three times. This is a new thing I have adopted, but I love that it reminds me to be thankful.

Adopting an air of gratitude in my quiet moments and alone with myself has increased my gratitude to others. I say thank you more easily and frequently to other people, to my children, friends and colleagues. I have noticed that my children are repeating gratitude language in their everyday lives. They have become so polite and I am so proud of them for listening.

We can infect other people with our gratitude. Take this example of being a parent – they are always watching what we say and do. Us adopting a gratitude attitude that they also take on board can encourage them to become kinder and more thoughtful to others.

In a relationship, kindness and gratitude towards your partner can encourage a more balanced, harmonious response reflected back to you. Though having come from an unbalanced long-term relationship, I am aware that there isn't always that reciprocal response from some partners.

How do you feel when someone expresses an appreciation for the work you did in your business or job? At work, if a manager or boss in the company shows appreciation to their employees, the likelihood is that the employee will feel inclined to return the respect and try harder to achieve in their work. In turn, that more focused effort could be noticed, recognised and rewarded by their superior or manager.

Being grateful has thus created a knock-on, pay back affect within the company, creating more balance and a better working environment for everyone.

Therefore, gratitude improves your outlook on life and can have a positive effect on those around you and your career/job. Being grateful or saying thank you costs nothing, and it is simple and incredibly effective.

EXERCISE 6: GRATITUDE TRAINING FOR THE MIND

- Keep a gratitude journal. This is a simple way to chart your gratitude lists and creates a positive mindset. It also acts as a physical reminder to think of things to be grateful for.

- Wake up each morning and state 5-10 things you are grateful for.

- When you are feeling low, stuck or negative, try saying 'thank you' three times in a row.

- Each day, tell someone something you appreciate about them. Make someone's day.

- Give. By giving back, even if it's letting someone jump the queue before you in the supermarket, it's reflecting an air of gratitude and graciousness. People do pay it back to others. Start a ripple effect, no matter how small.

- Be grateful for what you already have, but also thankful for what you hope is coming.

- Try not to ponder on what you lack, but instead on what you have. Living in lack leaves us thirsty in the desert. Bring an oasis into your life with the joy of giving thanks.

- Before going to sleep at night, repeat the morning's gratitude list of 5-10 things you are grateful for. Or simply say *thank you*.

Just try it. You have nothing to lose!

Chapter Summary

1. The power of language – How we communicate is key to how we communicate ourselves to the world.

2. Negative self-talk and negative thoughts have the power to create a destructive impact on our mind and body health.

3. Changing your inner dialogue by use of tools, tips and techniques.

4. Silence your inner critic.

5. How using positive language in your self-talk can positively impact your mind and body.

6. Creating more positive self-talk can improve your outlook on life and your perception of life in general. This in turn positively impacts the world around you

7. The power of gratitude; how being grateful can reduce a lack mentality and improve the way we view our lives.

8. The benefits of adopting an 'attitude of gratitude'.

9. Training our minds to be grateful reduces the feeling of lack and negativity and positively affects others around us.

Case Study 9: AK's Story – Addiction and Self Destructive Thoughts

The impact of negative, self-destructive thoughts turned me to drink and drugs as a soul anesthetic.

From as early as 8 I had worked out what I needed to escape from reality. I was a child that feared my own thoughts, and was happiest when sedated. Quickly I worked out that creating my own pain not only gave me attention, but also a whole load of prescription drugs, including sleepers.

I thought very little of myself whilst growing up, mainly because I believed no one else did. Although something I did know was that I was an amazing actress, and with this skill I could manipulate situations to my advantage. Money, men, drugs and alcohol. If I wanted something, I'd find a way, but not a healthy way.

I had learnt from such an early age that negative thoughts, in the short term, using various forms of monopolization, got me the high or low that I needed. Sadly, this only led me down a path of destruction. On many occasions I have lost everything, including properties, cars, friends and even my son (age 5).

The thing is, I felt comfort while under the influence. I never felt lonely, sad or depressed. Drugs and alcohol had become my best friend. I didn't see what those around me saw. On the outside I had nice clothes, my makeup and nails always looked perfect, and I held down jobs, often ones of high acclaim.

So on the outside I appeared to be a confident high achiever. The sad thing is that on the inside, I wasn't. Each day I would wake, and my first thoughts would be "Oh no not another day". I was filled with anxiety and a deep depression: "Do I really have to do this all over again?" I'd get up, put the kettle on, light a cigarette and within a few minutes I'd taken a few codeine with a glass of wine, and possibly a spliff. Working for myself, and not having to leave the house, this became a daily occurrence.

I also had a husband, who was also an addict, which didn't help matters. Not only did it mean drugs and alcohol were readily available, he was also a narcissist. So no matter who I was, or what I said or even dressed like, he would criticize and talk over me. In fact, he never even heard me most of the time. He would punish me regularly with little things, like ignoring me, never hugging me when he got into bed, blanking my texts or calls.

As you can imagine this led me down a path of negative self-talk. I had lost who I was; the pain inside was so intense. I actually started losing my mind, and thought if I didn't pull myself together I would be sectioned. I didn't listen to my own thoughts. I drank more and began sedating myself with amitriptyline. These would knock me out the second my head hit the pillow.

This went on for months, until one day I woke up shaking so violently that I was unable to walk in a straight line. I was so frightened and knew I was done. I just wanted to die. I had spent over 40 years of my life running away from my feelings and trying so hard to push my negative thoughts about myself away, just not in the right way.

I knew I was a kind and caring person. My life was full of amazing friends and wonderful opportunities. I'd travelled the world, and experienced so much. I just no longer saw a future.

At this point I curled into a ball on my sofa and screamed with tears; really hot tears, and they just wouldn't stop. Then I began to pray. I prayed and then called on of my best friend. He came immediately. From his massive hug, I calmed and remembered a saying I see every day in my kitchen: Thoughts become things. In my prayers I asked God to guide me, and help me get clean and sober.

From that dark, dark day, my prayers were answered. I am now in recovery and each day begins with positive thoughts, affirmations and gratitude.

I am finally on the road to recovery, and now when something negative comes into my head I don't pick up a drink or a drug. I go for a walk, call a friend or mediate. I am learning to like me for who I am and not the person that was created by chemical abuse.

If I can, anyone can.

~ Much love, AK xx

CHAPTER 5

TRAIT 4: **KNOW YOUR VISION**

'In order to carry a positive action, we must develop here a positive vision.'

~ Dalai Lama

Do you have a goal? Is there something you are working to achieve, or something you have always wanted to do but didn't have the time, encouragement or initiative to pursue? Or perhaps you have lacked the confidence to pursue your dreams? Well, now may be the time to take some positive steps towards pursuing that suppressed dream or vision.

When I was a young teenager sitting on top of a mountain with my dog, reflecting on stuff and escaping a chaotic home life for a few blessed hours, I had a sense of who I was and the person I wanted to be. I was going to become a writer and an artist and maybe have a little business. I would live in a cute little basement flat or small terrace house somewhere. My dreams weren't huge. In fact, looking back, they were pretty modest. At the time in my humble situation, they seemed significant and made me happy.

I lived in a small village town in the heart of the Welsh valleys. Famous people were posters on my walls or images on the television. Yet I knew deep inside me, at around fourteen or fifteen years of age, that I was going to do something amazing with my life one day. I didn't know what; I just had a feeling.

Then life took hold of me roughly and shook those dreams and goals the hell out of me. One by one, for the next thirty years, I watched them fall and rot like apples to the ground.

The past few years have seen those rotten apples bear fruit and shoot into tiny buds from the ground in which they lay sheltered and buried for all those years. This analogy reminds me of the growth of the bamboo tree. You may know the story.

- A farmer plants a bamboo seed in the ground and waters it.
- A year goes by and nothing happens. The farmer continues to water the ground where he planted the seed.
- Another year goes by and no shoots appear. The farmer continues to water the ground.
- Another year passes and still the farmer waters without seeing the growth.
- A fourth year passes and the farmer is patiently watering and tending to the area around the planted bamboo.
- Year five arrives and shoots appear.
- The bamboo takes just six weeks to grow to over 80 feet tall.

Question...how long did the bamboo take to grow?

If you answered six weeks, think about it. In reality, it took over five years to grow. Hidden beneath the soil, the bamboo's roots were growing and spreading out to ensure the bamboo tree could be supported when it finally pushed through and upward. It took five years before the roots were in a position to hold the weight of the tree. Philosopher Lao Tzu said, *'To see things in the seed, that is genius.'*

Our dreams are like this. They have to first be planted, then nurtured and continually fed before we begin to see the shoots appear. It takes patience and determination to watch your goals develop from a thought or desire into a reality. How many of us have a plan, a goal or a vision, only to give up when life sweeps our feet away? Or we buckle from the effects of negative words or criticism; or give up when we fail to see the progress of the fruits of our input? The message is that it takes time. Successful people still fail and sometimes even quit, but they get back up, back on their feet and back to working on their goals.

There are many statistics on the amount of millionaires who were once declared bankrupt, but then rose up again and reached the top. These are just a few: Abraham Lincoln, Walt Disney, George Foreman, singers Cyndi Lauper, M.C. Hammer and Elton John, Henry Ford, actress Kim Basinger, H.J. Heinz (of Heinz brand name), Larry King, director Francis Ford Coppola, actors Burt Reynolds and Randy Quaid, showman P.T. Barnum, blogger Perez Hilton. And Donald Trump...

As I write today, the Coronavirus is globally gripping and terrifying the world. I have temporarily lost all sources of income along with so many people around me. Working in the TV, film, fashion and media industry, us creative workers are being hit hard. Family incomes are being completely wiped out. How do you keep your vision going when this happens? How do I, as a single parent with no current income, keep my own dreams alive?

The answer is to **keep believing** in your dreams, regardless. Life goes on. It may take a while for individuals, families, businesses and economies to get back up after this global catastrophe is over, but the key is to keep watering that seed. Visualise the end result. I will talk more about visualisation later in this chapter.

So how does one do that when faced with financial ruin, or illness, or life being turned completely inside out and unrecognisable to what it once was? Without focusing on this virus and the impact it is having and will have on the world (because I know there will be numerous books written about it, plays, films, etc., in the future), I am only snapshotting a glimpse at it here. It's a dream snatcher; a vision killer and a goal thief, yes, but only if we allow it. My role in writing this book is to help guide you towards skills that can help move yourself out of whatever uncomfortable, stuck or unhappy place you may be in right now and to give you some tips and tricks to move yourself closer towards your goals and thus changing your life. Before the Covid-19 virus impacted the world so dramatically, the same reactions and emotions existed to trauma, sickness, loss and disappointment already affecting mankind. Right now, more people are experiencing these reactions and feelings than ever before. We are in a global crisis and how we react individually and as a collective is crucial.

Remember this saying and carry it in your heart, as I have the past four years since it was given to me:

'It isn't what happens to you, but how you react to it that matters.'

~ Epictetus, Greek Stoic Philosopher

Ask yourself this question...how do you respond?

STEP 1: Setting Your Goals

'When you are inspired by some great purpose, some extraordinary project, all your thoughts break their bonds.'

~ Patanjali, Ancient Philosopher

One of my more notable character traits, I believe, is my ability to always have a goal. This is key in moving yourself forward and highly successful people see the value in having a vision, dream or goals they wish to realise.

I love a goal!! Being a 'to do' and list making person, I have notepads filled with things to do, goals, notes on books I've read and plans, plans and more plans. I am a dreamer and a list maker.

For the past two years, I have started each New Year with a list of five main goals. I break each goal into sub goals – baby steps to achieve that particular goal. Two years ago, I achieved a small amount of my written goals or at least contributions towards them. Last year I achieved all but one of them (my personal goal). This year my goals are huge. I am currently making my way through them, despite facing the possibility of months at home with the kids. The world may be going into lockdown, but I am not. I have goals to achieve. I have a vision and plans to realise my dreams. This is the difference between existing and living. This is one of the greatest traits of a successful person – keeping your dream alive despite all that tries to crush them. In the words of the Dalai Lama,

'The goal is not to be better than the other man, but your previous self.'

So what did I do? What have I done to achieve this positive mindset towards goal planning and keeping a vision alive? These are my tips:

1. Know your goal
2. Write it down
3. Set a timeframe to achieve the goal
4. Break it down into small, focused steps
5. Affirm your goal daily
6. Carry your goal around with you – purse, wallet, bag, pocket

The most important point to remember is this – know precisely what you want. What do you want to achieve? Is it a job, a place, a possession, a fitter body, a higher mindset, a person/partner? What is your goal?

I have six goals. Why six? Because for me, I have six areas in my life that I want to achieve in. Here is a list of my top six goals:

My Goals 2020

1. Writing - Publish my writing projects
2. Art - Paint twenty angel oil paintings ready for an exhibition and print my angel greeting cards. Sell my artwork and become an international artist
3. Become a speaker and interviewer
4. Work - Become a highly paid makeup artist
5. Finances - Be completely self-sufficient and debt free
6. Love - Meet my life partner

These are pretty huge goals, but as Michelangelo, Renaissance painter and sculptor, famously stated,

'The greater danger for most of us is not that our aim is too high and we miss it, but that it is too low and we reach it.'

These are pretty powerful words.

~~~~~~~~~~

So what are the best ways to set a goal? Firstly, let's take a look at the five different types of goals and examples of what these goals might look like.

'Belief. The key is self-belief. Never stop believing in your vision, your goal an in YOU.'

Types of Goals

1. C type goal
2. Lifetime goal
3. Long term goal
4. Short term goal
5. Stepping stone goal

The C Type Goal

This is the penultimate goal. The goal that keeps you up at night; that reach for the moon dream you have, that 'if I could do, be, have anything' type of goal that lights up your face and makes your heart pound with excitement when you think about it. Add this goal to the four types of goals. This is the one that takes your breath away with excitement when you think about it!

Lifetime Goal

This is a goal that has no time span and can take from tomorrow to forever to achieve. Some examples: to become a better person, to achieve peace in life, to be happy, to live a wealthy life, to climb Everest, win an Oscar, visit the Seven Wonders of the World, earn a million pounds/dollars, meet a life partner, to one day meet Steven Spielberg/Oprah or any other inspirational famous personality.

Long Term Goal

Usually a 2-10 year goal plan. For example, study to become an architect, train to run a marathon or triathlon or another major sporting achievement, develop a million pound business, save to purchase a property, save for your child's wedding, start and run a successful business, achieve a degree, master's or PhD, become well known for your creative achievements, be a great role model for your children, be debt free.

Short Term Goal

These are typically short achievement goals, for example 0-12 months. They are short step goals to achieving your long or lifetime goals. Examples: applying for a college course or business loan, buying art materials to paint, increasing your social media output or following, enrolling in a gym or starting exercise classes, commencing a diet, arranging a meeting, making that call, joining a dating site, start budgeting or open up a savings account, be on time for appointments, school run, and meetings, read more books, get up earlier, etc.

Stepping Stone Goal

These are transitioning, action steps to take towards bigger goals. Examples are similar to the short-term goals. Think of them as baby steps.

For example, call your bank to consolidate debt, apply for another job, take good photos for your dating profile, buy weights to work out at home, find an interest-free credit card option, know the transport timetable, order workout gear.

EXERCISE 8: YOUR GOALS

Know your goal or goals and list them, then try this exercise. It may help you to focus on achieving a goal that has been kicking around in your head for a while. Remember that achieving a goal is a process, but unless you start to make steps towards that goal, then how will you know if you are capable of achieving it or not? The best time to start is now.

In your notebook, or on a blank sheet of paper or in this book (I have left space below), write down the five types of goals. Then write out your goals under each goal heading. For example:

GOAL TYPE	GOAL
C TYPE GOAL	e.g. Run a multi-million pound/dollar business
LIFE TIME GOAL	e.g. Earn a million pounds
LONG TERM GOAL	e.g. Run a successful business in...
SHORT TERM GOAL	e.g. Enrol in a business course/get a job in...
STEPPING STONE GOAL	e.g. Find a suitable course

MY GOALS...

Now write down your goals here.

STEP 2: Creating A Vision Board

If you have never created a vision board before or even know what it is, let me explain why I have included its importance in this book. According to Wikipedia,

'A dream board or vision board is a collage of images, pictures, and affirmations of one's dreams and desires, designed to serve as a source of inspiration and motivation, and to use the law of attraction to attain goals.'

A vision board is a visual tool used to create your specific goals and dreams. By using images, pictures and words on board, card or by using an area on your wall called a 'vision wall', you create visual pictures of the things you wish to materialise in your life.

I have found them extremely useful in my life and each year I create a new vision board and add or change it as the year progresses and my goals get achieved or changed.

Why Create A Vision Board?

A vision or dream board provides focus and clarity. For example, if you want to one day fall in love and get married, then post the words 'Love' and 'Mr & Mrs' with pictures of hearts and wedding bouquet flowers and photos of a couple, or your favourite style of wedding dress.

Got a business idea? Then post a goal plan with words, pictures or affirmations. If writing a book is your goal, then print out pictures or images of writers/books and specific words. Or use post it notes or postcards with affirmations or positive words such as 'Winner' or 'Success' or 'Don't Quit'.

John Assaraf, an entrepreneur, philanthropist, teacher and

international speaker, recalled his own experience with the use of vision boards. In 1995, he created a vision board with all of his dreams and desires. It was a collection of images and pictures that represent how he wanted his ideal life to look. In 2000, after recently moving home, his son brought in a box. In that box, he discovered the vision board he had created five years previous. To his astonishment, the picture of his dream house that he had pinned onto the 1995 vision board, was the very same house he was now living in. It wasn't just a similar house, but the exact SAME house he had pictured five years previous. Such is the power of using visionary tools such as a vision board.

Here is a mental picture of my vision board.

I have a photo of Oprah Winfrey in the centre, because she inspires me and I want to become as strong an inspiration to others as she is to me. I also dream to present and interview and become a speaker one day. That's a long-term goal, since I am already on that journey and it's a matter of time before I get closer to realising that goal. I have the words 'I Am Empowerment' on either side of Oprah's photo. Underneath these words are pictures of my favourite speakers – Les Brown, Lisa Nichols and Maya Angelou. These are my role models. I also want to meet Les, Lisa and Oprah one day (Maya has passed). Being empowered is very important to me. Perhaps you may want to put a role model on your board as I have done.

Underneath these are pictures and words dedicated to my lifetime goal of being a celebrity makeup artist, including the word 'Vogue'. Since I currently also work on fashion editorials, I would love to have my work featured in Vogue. I currently have seven magazine publications with my work featured, but Vogue is definitely a lifetime goal.

At the top left on my vision board are pictures of a white house, home interiors and words such as *dream home*. I currently rent, and one day would love to own my own home. That's a lifetime goal. A short-term goal for me would be to rent a larger home whilst I build up to the realisation of that bigger achievement.

There's also a photo of my two favourite dogs which I one day hope to have as pets. My nine year old son is desperate for a dog, yet I know there are current restrictions in my life before I can justify having a dog and being more at home. My long-term goal is to achieve just that.

The top right of my vision board is dedicated to my personal goal – to meet my life partner. It has the words love in various forms scattered across and a printout of a quote and a poem I have written.

Below that are my writing goals. I have written 'Times Best Seller List' and 'Amazon Best Seller List'. These are definitely lifetime goals for me. To have my work be highly recognised internationally would definitely be a dream come true.

Then come my art goals on the bottom right. I create oil paintings of angels and recently registered myself as 'Painter of Angels'. I have put this on the vision board as my lifetime goal is to become an internationally recognised artist. In fact, I sold a painting to a guy in New York three months ago. So I am on the path towards realising that goal as a reality.

So that's a vision board. All you require is a board such as a pin, cork or firm board of some kind. You can pick up corkboard pins from most stationery shops. Then browse magazines and newspapers for words and images, or research images on your computer and print them out. Use photographs, post it notes or anything you want to pin to the board to affirm that goal. It can be pretty and structured, or chaotic and random. It doesn't matter: it's your goals and dreams being expressed into a visual tool to encourage and focus you. It's your mental vision for yourself being expressed physically.

'In order to carry a positive action, we must develop a positive vision.'

~ Dalai Lama

So now that you have decided what your goals are, broken them down into types of goals and given them a timeline, it is time to take steps towards actioning these goals. And the first place to start is to create a visual image of those goals so you can be inspired daily and not lose hope when life throws some pretty hard lemons at you!

EXERCISE 9: CREATE A VISION BOARD

For this exercise, you will require the following materials.

1. Your list of goals
2. Large A3 or A2 card, or a pin board or cork board
3. Pins, sticky tape
4. Postcards with affirmations or positive words
5. Post it notes
6. Print or cut out pictures, images or words that represent your goal

Now go create!

So now that you have your goals and your vision board to affirm and give visual power to those goals, let's take a look at the power of affirmations and how they can also help you achieve and realise your ambitions and dreams.

STEP 3: Affirmations

Claude M. Bristol author the book of the book 'The Magic of Believing' (Pocket Books 1948), wrote,

'It's the repetition of affirmations that leads to belief. And once that belief becomes a deep conviction, things begin to happen.'

Affirmations are positive and uplifting words, phrases or sentences used to focus one's mind on achieving something specific, or for encouragement. They can be repeated regularly and said with confidence and conviction to enhance a message you want yourself to hear.

Since the mind doesn't know the difference between what is real and what is fantasy, the use of an affirmation can program the mind into believing those words are the truth. For example, saying 'I am loved' over and over can take away a feeling of loneliness or lack. It was one of the affirmations I found hardest to say at first, when I started my mindset change journey a few years ago, because I truly didn't love myself. I can now say it with conviction since I do believe I love me. I know others love me too, but I had to truly know I loved myself first and foremost.

There are different types of affirmations. Some are specific to your goal, your feeling of lack, your work, your finances, or your love life. Some are I AM affirmations, which tend to be quite short and some are affirming sentences or phrases to repeat. There are morning affirmations, gratitude affirmations, affirmations targeted at specific areas of your life, e.g. beauty, intelligence, strength, health, friendships, love, connections, and work. If you require more income, you can use an affirmation to program your mind that you are wealthy and abundant and earning 'X' amount a year, or that

'X' will flow to you. There are affirmations for children and young adults to use, affirmations to improve confidence and self-esteem, and even affirmations to heal from pain, illness and heartache.

An affirmation works because the subconscious mind does not know truth from fantasy. If you are not aware of the difference between subconscious and conscious thinking, then here is a brief summary.

Sigmund Freud, the founder of psychoanalysis, held a theory that the mind was constructed of three parts – the conscious, the preconscious and the subconscious. He illustrated it with the picture of an iceberg. The tip, or one seventh of the iceberg above the water, is our **conscious** mind. Below the waterline, was a layer called the **preconscious** mind and the bulk of the iceberg under that layer, was the **subconscious** mind.

Let's take that image and imagine the three parts of our mind like this:

Conscious Mind

This contains all the thoughts, emotions, feelings, and

memories experienced at a present time. It's the rational part of our mind. For example, you bang your hand and it hurts and your other hand will no doubt comfort it and you wince in pain.

Preconscious Mind

This is any thought or action that could be brought into the conscious mind. They are unconscious thoughts that have the ability to be recalled at a moment. An example of this would be a name, a description or an address. Most memories are preconscious.

Subconscious Mind

This is the hidden depth of our thoughts and memories and experiences. Included in the subconscious are our fears and beliefs, often imposed on us from childhood or a very early age. The subconscious is like a filing cabinet of every thought, emotion, fear, memory and experience we have ever had. It's a very powerful part of our mind and if left to run our lives, can have a negative impact on our conscious decisions. An example of a subconscious thought is 'I don't fly because the plane might crash'. As we explored in a previous chapter on fears, the fear of flying is not a rational, conscious thought, but one influenced by a deep subconscious fear, possibly originating from something seen or said many years previously.

~~~~~~~~~~

The power of a positive affirmation allows us to overcome the negative impact of a subconscious thought by consciously affirming a different truth. If the subconscious mind cannot tell the difference between what is true and what is false, then it will listen to whatever it is told.

So then, if you have the subconscious belief that you are not intelligent, because someone once called you stupid at school (eg. a teacher once told me, aged twelve, that I had 'stupid eyes' – that affected me for a long time afterwards), using an affirmation can change that. A typical affirmation to counteract the belief of being stupid would be:

'I am an intelligent communicator. I have a depth of knowledge and can intelligently process information. I am intelligent.'

Note that only positive words were used in this affirmation. Not once was there a reference to the word 'stupid'. Affirmations should be clear, and above all, focused. They are used to convince the subconscious mind that the words you speak are the truth.

The reason it is suggested that we repeat affirmations over and over, is to convince our subconscious mind that we are telling it the truth. We have to retrain the way we think and change the words we speak. That's why I wrote previous chapters on the use of negative versus positive words and thoughts. If you keep telling yourself you are stupid because that's what your hidden belief is, then your mind will not believe otherwise and that will be your understanding of yourself. But if you change your words to 'I am intelligent', eventually, your mind will believe that to be the truth instead.

Do you now see how powerful our words are? You can cut someone in two with harsh words, or you uplift them and make their day with words of love, encouragement and kindness. It is no different to how we communicate with ourselves. I hope you are getting the message that you have the power to change your life through how you communicate with yourself? Earl Nightingale, American author and radio speaker, said, *'We become what we think about.'* As mentioned before, how we think can determine what we do and how we live our lives.

'The intellect has little to do on the road to discovery. There comes a leap in consciousness, call it intuition or what you will, and the solution comes to you, and you don't know how or why.'

~ Albert Einstein, Physicist

The Power of Affirmations

So now that we have established the three aspects of our mind and the power of communication to ourselves and to others, let's return to the power of affirmations.

Here are some examples of I AM affirmations that may be useful to you:

I am loved
I am enough
I am successful
I am happy
I am beautiful
I am Divine
I am a great mother (wife/friend/daughter etc.)
I am learning to let go of fear
I am healing
I am not alone
I am allowed to feel good about myself
I am a warrior
I am a survivor
I am feminine

I am worthy
I am on the right path and moving in the right direction
I am powerful
I am strength
I am trusting the process
I am believing that I am loved
I am forgiving myself
I am courageous
I am prosperous
I am abundant
I am grateful
I am a leader

This is just a small sample and I am sure you can add, adapt and expand these to be specific for you.

Examples of Affirmations for Improving Self-Esteem

I feel good about myself
I am good enough
I am enough
I am working on being the best possible me
I accept myself
I'm happy being me
My life is meaningful
I feel good about being me
I love the real me
I am perfectly me
The more I accept and love myself, the more I accept and love others
My self-esteem is growing daily
I am confident in my abilities
I am valuable
I am magnificent
I am worthy of good things
There is no one better to be than myself
I am not other people's opinions of me

Affirmations for a Positive Attitude and Mindset

I am proud of myself
My challenges help me grow
I feel joy and contentment in my life right now
I embrace happiness and deserve to feel happy
I accept who I am
I'm becoming a better person every day
I find joy and contentment in most things I do
I love my life
I love who I am and who I am becoming
My heart is overflowing with joy
I am amazing and I can do anything
I am prepared to succeed
I fill my mind with positive thoughts
I choose to see the positive and the good
Today is a great day
I create the life I want to live
I will accomplish great things today
I believe in me
My possibilities are endless
You got this girl/boy
I am brave, bold and beautiful
I will not worry about things I cannot control
My thoughts become my reality

There are so many different types of affirmations you can say. If you are new to this, then choose three to five to begin with that resonate with you. Say them daily and repeat as often as you can. If you really want to change your mindset, set a reminder on your phone to repeat the affirmation like a mantra at certain times throughout the day, for example, morning, lunchtime and before bed.

You could also write them on post it notes or cards and dot them around the house. How about taking on board this advice that the celebrity hypnotherapist and therapist Marissa Peer suggests in her videos, books and talks: Take a red felt tip marker or lipstick and write the three words, I AM ENOUGH, across a mirror. I did this a few months ago and wrote it on the bathroom mirror, on my daughter's mirror and on mine. Mine is still up there (I do clean my mirrors, but cleaned around that inscription!). I have had to call on those words as my makeup work started to cancel or postpone due to the impact of the virus on the fashion, media, TV and film industry. The reminder that I am enough, despite the lack of work and income causing me to doubt that fact, was a great reminder.

Do not underestimate the power of positive words and affirmations. They can change your life because they change your thoughts. If you change the way you think, the world around you also starts to change and then the real changes in your own life will become evident. Doors of opportunity previously closed to you will miraculously open. Relationships around you will change, or you may let go of connections that no longer serve a more positive you. Watch as new connections come to you that reflect the person you are becoming. It is important to remember that we attract what we are. So if you want to attract more positive people and situations around you, then focus on becoming that which you seek.

Here is a mantra that I repeat daily to attract what I want into my life:

'That which I am seeking, is also seeking me.'

I have also adapted it to attract the partner into my life that I desire (goal six):

'He whom I am seeking, is also seeking me.'

STEP 4: Meditation

This quote from the Bahagdav Gita in 'The Song of God', a 700 verse Hindu scripture from the epic Mahabharata by Vyasa, says:

'When meditation is mastered, the mind is unwavering like the flame of a candle in a windless place.'

So what is meditation and why would it be useful to you for achieving your vision or goal? First and foremost, there is so much noise around us and also in our heads that we sometimes need to stop, turn off that noise and go deep within. According to Wikipedia, mediation is useful *'to train attention and awareness, and achieve a mentally clear and emotionally calm and stable state'.*

When I first began to practise meditation, I really struggled to focus. I would sit as instructed on the floor, with my back straight, legs crossed and feet tucked under and the palms of my hands open to receive. But my mind raced. It was so overfull of racing thoughts crashing against the walls of my brain and banging into each other in the process, that I could just not focus. In the guided meditation I listened to, it gave instructions to see the distracting thought as a balloon in my head and to acknowledge it and send the thought balloon on its way. Well, to begin with, my brain was so overfull of thoughts, I felt like my head would lift with all the balloons in my mind!

Then a friend told me to focus on a candle. I should stare

at the candle and then close my eyes. Still the thoughts came. I am a complete over thinker so emptying my mind of thoughts was so difficult for me. So he suggested I not close my eyes completely, but leave them half shut and continue to look at the candle. However, since I was always so tired being a single parent of three children and juggling two small businesses and a part time job at the time, I was nervous about falling asleep with a candle in front of me.

Another meditation practising friend suggested I focus on a mark on the wall and keep my eyes half open, since closing my eyes only brought more thoughts into my busy mind. This worked for me. If I fell asleep, which I often did, then it was safer.

If you have never practised meditation before, be prepared for it to take some time before you get it working for you. It is a practise after all. But stick with it, because it has proven for me to be one of the most relaxing and useful of all mindfulness practises that I have learned. Since meditation helps focus the mind deeply for a period of time, it is worth being patient and practising regularly to get the hang of it. Once you learn to implement it into your daily life, the benefits of mediation are significantly rewarding.

There are seven types of mediation: mindfulness meditation, transcendental meditation, guided meditation, Vipassana Meditation, Loving Kindness Meditation, chakra meditation and yoga meditation. For the purpose of this introduction to meditation, I will just focus on the first three. All involve the practise of sitting in a comfortable position, back straight and eyes closed. There are different types of meditation poses, but for simplicity I have illustrated two below, one on the floor and one sitting on a chair or stool.

Simple Breathing Meditation Exercise

There are various breathing exercises to do when one meditates. For the benefit of simplicity, we will focus on just one - using a three breath in and out method. When positioned for meditation as in the illustration above if possible and with eyes closed, breathe in for a count of three, hold the breath for three and release for three. Repeat this three times until the breath regulates as normal. This breathing exercise focuses the mind, brings oxygen into the mind and body and relaxes us to begin the meditation. When comfortable with meditation, then you can increase the length of time for breathing in, holding and breathing out, preferably only up to a count of ten. Passing out before beginning the meditation will not be very beneficial!

Mindfulness Meditation

This meditation enables us to be aware of our thoughts and emotions. When in this meditation, we focus on tuning our thoughts into what we are feeling in the moment. It is a focus on mental imagery and an awareness of the body in the moment. It is a wonderful way to focus an overthinking mind and training thoughts to stay put. Begin the meditation with the breathing exercise.

Transcendental Meditation

This is a meditation using a mantra or word such as 'Om' repeatedly. It has a suggested practise period of twenty minutes. Begin the meditation with the breathing exercise.

Guided Meditation

This is a meditation process that involves either a teacher or form of guidance from a sound recording or video, such as a YouTube video. It involves the use of visualisation through imagery, sounds, textures and smells, creating mental pictures. Begin the meditation with the breathing exercise.

Look up these different types of meditation and chose one that feels right for you.

'Silence is a true friend who never betrays.'
~ Confucius, Ancient Philosopher

When I first started practising meditation, the most helpful style of mediation to train my overthinking monkey mind into a mindful space was using the guided meditation technique. I would find a short video clip (5-10 minutes) on YouTube and tune in. I also got a free meditation app on my phone, which documented my mediations and offered a range of short or longer meditations on a range of different emotions or areas of focus. Just before I began to fully engage in meditation practises, I was experiencing low, negative moods and intermittent anxiety over loss of income and rising debt, I discovered that the use of guided imagery meditations, along with the focused meditations on my phone app, were extremely helpful to help release those anxious feelings.

Now, because I have been practising meditation for around three years, I can close my eyes, breathe and meditate without the requirement of guidance. I have mastered the practise of going deep within myself and centering my thoughts and have learnt how to empty my mind and enjoy a peaceful, mindful state. I also find that during meditation, ideas come to me, or I receive answers to questions I pose myself.

Currently, with the world on lockdown and in self-isolation, what is our response? Panic and go nuts from lack of freedom and distraction, or balance ourselves by going within and figuring out who we are and what we are capable of? I choose the latter. The first one drove me to the snacking cupboard and the last thing I want right now is having to get rid of a half stone of over eating weight on top of figuring myself out in these unprecedented times. So every day I meditate and feel the peace. This morning I set an intention before my meditation (on my bed with the sun pouring onto my face through the window). I asked 'What can I do to change my financial situation created by the loss of earnings in this crisis?' I sat and breathed. My eyes were closed and the sun on my face was warming me from head to toe. An image came to me of creating video content by myself and also with my daughter. What I received was a vision of how I could respond to this crisis; what my personal response could be.

Visualisation is my weapon for keeping my hopes alive. It

is the fuel that feeds my passion and vision, and inspires me to want more and do more with my life.

STEP 5: Visualisation

'Visualisation is everything. If you can imagine something you can do it. Nothing happens in reality until it happens in your mind first.'

~ Jim Carrey, Actor

Visualisation is something I discovered whilst reading works by authors and thinkers such as Jack Canfield, Dr Joe Vitale, Erckhart Tolle and Dr Wayne Dyer. Yet for a long time, I fought using it as a practise for my own life.

I have always been a thinker and indeed, the main criticism I receive from others who know me well has been that I overthink everything (so true). I have a Bachelor of Honours degree in Philosophy, and after my studies I turned down a PhD that would have enabled me to apply to become a philosophy lecturer. I didn't turn it down because I didn't want to do it, as I would have loved the opportunity, but because I needed to work to survive and could not afford the tuition fees. As a natural storyteller, I started writing in my mid-twenties, yet stopped when the book I submitted to publishers was continually rejected. I gave up easily back then. Now I keep trying until I find a solution. I lost confidence in my writing abilities and life stepped in and took over.

Yet I have always enjoyed daydreaming, since I was a little girl. It's been a safe place for me during crazy and tumultuous times growing up. I would dream of meeting pop stars, of dancing in musicals, of seeing my art in people's homes and maybe even one day becoming a writer. But I let these dreams go for so many years. It wasn't until I began a network marketing business that I started to focus on self-development. That led to reading mindset improvement books and listening to audio books in the car, or when cooking or doing chores in the house.

Then, when life was completely crazy three years ago, I started listening to three speakers on YouTube – Dr Wayne Dyer, the inspirational speaker Lisa Nichols and the motivational speaker Les Brown. Every day I would play these guys whenever possible. Short video clips to uplift and focus me. Or I would put on a motivational YouTube that would verbally kick my butt into believing I could be, do or have whatever I want. Thanks to the motivation I was getting, I started to think more about what could be possible for my life. I up-scaled my ambitions and the vision for my future. It was around that time I re-discovered the joys of daydreaming, or, as these great thinkers and speakers would say, I started to visualise.

~~~~~~~~~~

It is possible to materialise what we desire into our lives by focusing on it already existing. If you really want to change your life, try visualisation as a tool. It is more powerful than you realise and used by many people. Arnold Schwarzenegger, Hollywood actor, film producer, statesman and former body builder, said,

'Create a vision of who you want to be, and then live into that picture as if it were already true.'

EXERCISE 5: THE PEAR

Try this exercise. Sit down. Get comfortable. Breathe in deeply. Close your eyes and focus. Ready?

Okay, now open your hand, either hand and palm facing up. I've placed a pear in your hand. Can you feel it? It's a big, juicy green pear.

Bring the pear up to your nose and smell it. Can you smell the delicious pear aroma? It's ripe and ready to eat. Yummy.

Now take a bite. Yes, go on, take a bite. Isn't it delicious and refreshing? The juice from the pear is escaping your lips and running down your chin. If you're not careful, it's going to drip on your top.

Now open your eyes.

Did you feel the pear in your hand? Did you imagine taking a bite and tasting the succulent white flesh? Could you smell the pear aroma? Did you imagine the juice dropping down your chin? Perhaps your mouth salivated at the thought of eating the pear?

This is visualisation.

If you experienced those sensations, then you have just witnessed firsthand the power of visualisation. The pear in reality does not exist in physical form, but you created an image in your mind so powerful that it gave you the illusion that the pear existed.

Now, take one of your goals and create the same experience. Close your eyes and this time imagine the goal already realised. You have already achieved that goal. You have already accomplished that which you seek to achieve. Breathe in the acknowledgement that you already have it. Now, check in with your emotions. How do you feel? Are you sad or happy? What is the picture in your head? What is the mind movie that you just created in your mind?

In the mid-1900s, an American called Neville Goddard (1905-1972) spoke about the power of using imagination to realise a goal. Goddard, an author, prophet and teacher, believed that imagination is God and thus we all have God within us. Therefore, we have all the necessary tools and power within us to create the life we desire. He believed that through imagination, all things were possible. He believed that we are constantly creating our reality and that if we can remove the boundaries between imagination and that which we perceive to be real, then we are capable of creating the life we truly desire.

Just with the exercise of the pear, Goddard suggested the concept of attaching feelings to the idea of what we desire. He spoke of imagining the fulfilment of what we desire, or the 'end result' and the feelings of being in the moment of that achievement. That's the key to his theory; to imagine the feelings of achieving what is desired, the moment during or after achieving it. The emotion attached to the realisation of the goal makes the desire for the goal that much more powerful. The key is to repeat this exercise over and over until the feeling attaches itself to the image, in order for us to believe that we are truly capable of fulfilling that goal or desire.

The last step in Goddard's theory was to let go of the outcome and to accept and KNOW that you have already achieved that which you seek. This took me a while to figure out and get to grips with. I could not believe it could be that easy. According to Goddard's theory, I simply had to believe that I already had those things I most desired. Truthfully, I fought it because it seemed too simple. Yet the more I practised doing this, the more I felt a part of the goal I desired.

The Process of Visualisation

1. Know your goal.
2. Tune into your goal and create a story in your mind of being in the present moment of achieving or already having achieved that goal.
3. Visualise the outcome.
4. Feel the feeling of having already fulfilled the goal.
5. Believe in this as a reality. Do not doubt.
6. Let go, surrender doubt and accept that this is the truth: that you have already achieved that which you are seeking.
7. Smile. It adds to the good feeling.
8. Repeat regularly.

Finally, remember that we have all the answers inside us. Everything we need already exists within. It's simply a question of quietening our mind, setting an intention and visualising what you want and imagining that you have already achieved it.

'Everything in the Universe is within you, ask all from yourself.'

~ Rumi

STEP 6: Understand the Law of Attraction

'What you have become, is what you have thought.'

~Immortal Buddha

There is a book called THE SECRET that I urge everyone to read, because it is a life changing book. It was written by the Australian author Rhonda Byrne in 2006. It is a self-help book focused on the belief that thoughts can directly affect and change a person's life. We have already discussed this in a previous chapter. THE SECRET is based on the idea of The Law of Attraction However, The Law of Attraction existed centuries before Byrne wrote about it. Buddha reflected, as above, that our thoughts make us what we are, and physicist Albert Einstein stated:

'The world as we have created it is a process of our thinking. It cannot be changed without changing our thinking.'

The Law of Attraction is the ability to attract into our lives what we really desire. Byrne and the Law of Attraction suggest that by focusing on the things we desire instead of those things we lack, we are able to manifest those desired things into our lives.

Have you ever had the situation where you decided to get a new car and you chose the model, design and colour, and then could not stop seeing that exact same car? Suddenly, that car is everywhere you look. Why does that happen? Is it a coincidence? This is a simplistic explanation of the Law of Attraction. We thought of the car, couldn't stop thinking of the car, and then the car materialises.

It's a very powerful tool to have in your mental tool kit. I am only briefly covering it here in this chapter, but I urge everyone to read Rhonda Byrne's book. I found it gave me a deeper understanding of the power of my mind and my mental capabilities through the use of focused thought. If we were to focus on the existence of the thing we wanted rather than the lack of it, then we have the opportunity to bring that thing into being. However, because our mind believes what it is told, if the lack thought is more dominant then we will continue to attract the lack into our lives, or at least keep the thing we want from appearing. Therefore, we need to keep our focus razor sharp on what we do want to appear in our lives rather than what we don't. Focus is the key, but focusing on the right thoughts.

'A man who chases two rabbits, catches neither.'
~ Ancient Chinese Proverb

Another interesting concept of The law of Attraction is that what you put out, you receive back. So if you are prone to being an angry, resentful and unhappy person, you tend to receive that back in your life. Some of you may be wondering right now why the things that have happened to you did? Well, I asked myself that many times over the past twenty-five years in particular. I cannot speak for you, but I do know that if I had this knowledge I am imparting to you a couple of decades ago, my life right now would probably be very different. However, I did not have the correct mindset in place to make the necessary changes in my life. My negative, self-depreciating thought processes created so many hurdles and obstacles in my life, that these concepts of change and enlightenment were difficult to attain. I had created huge walls around me through years of adopting and retaining a challenged view of my life. I mainly lived a life of restriction and self-imposed boundaries created by people, circumstance and a failure to open my eyes to adopting new responses.

When I read this Confucius quote, I realised that unless I chose to change my habits and attitudes, then my life wasn't going to change and I was going to remain in a stuck and unhappy place,

'Only the wisest and stupidest men never change.'

Taking the words of this quote literally, I wanted to develop greater wisdom rather than remain in my 'stupid' place.

Are you ready to change? Are you ready to take those steps towards a greater freedom in your life? Are you ready to realise your potential and become more than what you have settled for? It is your choice; it is always your choice. I urge you to choose wisely.

'The will to win, the desire to succeed, the urge to reach your full potential...these are the keys that will unlock the door to personal excellence.'

~ Confucius

Chapter Summary

1. Know your goals, write them down.
2. Look at your goals daily.
3. Create a vision board.
4. Create a list of affirmations that work for you to achieve your goal or create positivity.
5. Practise meditation. Choose a meditation style that works for you and remember that it takes practise.
6. Visualise achieving that goal – imagine what it feels like to already have that which you seek.
7. Add the power of Law of Attraction in your life.

Case Study 10: Ann – On Visualisation

Let me introduce myself; I am Ann Varney, a Spiritual Teacher and Therapist. I help people globally with Soul Loss, and I also teach people about spiritual modalities. I absolutely love what I do and love seeing the transformations that occur in people on a daily basis.

I also know a thing or two about visualisations and how powerful they can be if they are done correctly. I have many years of practice and on many occasions have experienced what many people would call the miraculous, as even I too have been in awe at some of the success I have had with visualisations.

I remember many years ago I was in a business that in the winter months was very low in income.

My cousin wanted to go to New York for her 50th birthday. Well, you can imagine I had all my bills to pay, my employees' wages to pay, Christmas in front of me and I had 2 sons to care for, as well as buying presents. Being a single mum, this was no easy task at Christmas for me.

I had 7 days to do everything and book a flight from Scotland, a hotel room and spending money as well as all the rest of the things I had to pay.

This is how I did it (and have done this many times in my life).

I made the decision I was going, and I then started to visualise my cousin and I on the plane, laughing and having a glass of wine. I saw myself getting off the airplane and going to our hotel room. I saw myself walking down Fifth Avenue, going to a show on Broadway, going to Tiffany's ... you get the drift; but I also saw myself being so happy doing this.

Some say it's not as easy as that. I know.... But I was determined. So every time the negative thoughts came and said I was stupid, "How the hell can you go? You can't even pay your bills", I would just think of me on the airplane and laughing; always laughing and feeling the joy, so I became excited like a teenager.

I packed my case and told everyone I was so happy to be going to New York. I just kept imagining me being there with my cousin and us both going to dinner for her birthday in a posh restaurant with a birthday cake. Wow! So I visualised this too.

I read THE SECRET on Christmas Day and I knew without a shadow of a doubt it was up to me if I would be in New York or not.

It was as if the Universe had my back as many strange occurrences happened simultaneously. It was as if my energy vibration changed into this excitable person instead of the worried, anxious person I was. All these ideas came into my mind, like to open my shop for 2 days between Christmas and New Year, which is something I never did.

What transpired is that 2 people placed an order for £2,700 each (the same wedding dress) and both people ordered it via telephone and email which was unheard of. They didn't even try it on and both paid in full, again unheard of.

To say I was ecstatic was an understatement. It was all the things I visualised and so much more.

So how did this happen in such a short space of time?

These are the steps I took:

I visualised it in great detail.

I believed without a shadow of doubt I was going - like a deep knowing (even though some negative thoughts came in). My behaviours reflected me going to New York - packing my suitcase and getting my sons taken care of.

I opened myself up to divine guidance and got out of my own way.

I flowed with creativity and abundant ideas and followed them.

I suggest when you would love to do something but something is stopping you, like money or not having someone to take care of your children, or anything else for that matter, I would tell you to follow the above steps with enough conviction and focused visualisations that you will succeed even more than your wildest expectations.

~ Ann Varney, a Spiritual Teacher and Therapist

Case Study 11: Kerry – On Meditation
Meditation is a Gift

Meditation has guided me out of destructive behaviour patterns and negative energies to a more authentic, peaceful me. It has helped strip away deeply embedded belief systems, shown me how to harness and channel a chaotically creative brain and how to discover joy.

In 1998 I moved to Manhattan and lived there for almost two years. It was an exciting and 'movie like' experience and I'm grateful to have called it home, even for that short time. I am a trained actress but, since I had no visa, working there wasn't an option. So, supported by my then husband, I studied in earnest: method acting, cabaret performance and photography. I was in a privileged position and I loved learning and experiencing the many gifts these art-forms afforded me.

There were exhilarating highs during this time; lots of them. But, despite my husband's support, I never felt contented or safe and I certainly never felt personal fulfilment. I was, to be honest, a nervous wreck and I constantly chastised that nervous wreck for feeling that way.

The acting profession was the perfect environment for nurturing my self-destruction. I'd had to work hard for any academic achievement at school but my acting talents had always generated a feeling of success. It was a relief to have found something I was congratulated for. Driven by a love of literature, a joy for singing and desire for more applause, I spent three terrifying years at drama school. You see, I had to hide dyslexia and chronic insecurity. I felt foundation-less, had a permanent ache in my throat from holding back tears and lived constant 'jazz hands mode'.

Years later, back in the UK, divorce and the prospect of losing out on motherhood brought me to emotional collapse, and after sixteen years in the acting profession, I finally decided to stop; to leave it, my identification with it and my love of its artistic processes, behind. I was exhausted and overcome by my sympathetic nervous system defaults. For months I barely left my house. I watched nonstop movies and I lived off little more than black coffee. I had relied upon the labels of 'actress' and 'trophy wife' for self-identification and rejecting both left me feeling a valueless failure. For years, I had been so focused on hiding an inadequate me and cultivating the mask of acceptability that I'd hijacked my own happiness.

I've learned that we are a product of our experiences and, indeed, those of our ancestors. I've learned that our deeply entrenched thought patterns dictate our actions and how we experience life.

But I've learned that these and our nervous system can be re-trained. When we understand that our challenges are gifts that shift our behaviour, and that there are tools for living if we learn to use them, the world becomes a fascination instead of merely an environment in which to survive. Meditation is one of those tools for living.

I now teach how to live. I teach yoga: a gift, a tool and a meditation for life. It's a journey. These days my monkey mind tends to evoke a wry smile in me rather than personal devastation and my greatest wish is to pass on how.

~ Kerry Emerson: Kerry@thelittleyogaplace.co.uk

CHAPTER 6

TRAIT 5: SAY YES TO EVERY OPPORTUNITY

'Opportunity knocks at the door only once.'

~ Ancient Chinese Proverb

Do not underestimate the power of saying yes to opportunity. In fact, within a few of my social groups, I am known as the 'Yes Girl'. Yet that wasn't always the case. I lived in fear for so many years: fear of change, of being seen, of letting go, of stepping out and fear of taking risks. After the work I did on letting go of my negative thoughts and self-talk, I was advised by my then mentor Richard Marchand to *'say yes to any opportunity and figure out the how after'*; so this is what I did. I adopted that mentality, but early on, I fought each opportunity that came my way, with every excuse I could think of:

'I don't have childcare'
'I can't afford to'
'I'm not qualified/experienced/trained'
'I lack confidence'
'I'm not good enough'
'I can't...I can't...I can't...'

You see, we can give ourselves any excuse we want, but the reality is that we are often fearful of what may happen if we do say *yes*. It's so easy to remain in our comfort zone rather than to step outside of the box and to take risks or the opportunity on offer.

'Small opportunities are often the beginning of great enterprises.'

~ Demosthens, Ancient Philosopher

As we say *yes* to opportunity and take steps towards our goals, some people around us may feel it's their right to try to stop us or criticise our attempts or ideas. This will be a time to trust your intuition or gut instinct. Your body will know when something is dangerous – I do not for one moment, suggest you do anything that would endanger your life or put yourself or others at risk. I am talking here about the naysayers hindering you from stepping outside of your comfort zone and trying something new. Whilst most people will support your desire to reach higher, develop yourself or take steps towards your goals, there will be some who will want to offer caution, or even be downright negative. Remember that it is always your choice. You get to choose the life you want.

Opportunity Knocks

It is worth recalling that at one point it was widely accepted that the earth was flat, until Columbus sailed around it and proved otherwise. Nobody thought space travel was possible, until men successfully landed on the moon. And don't forget the runner Roger Banister. He was the first man to run a mile in under 4 minutes at the 1952 Helsinki Olympics. Before then, it was thought impossible to achieve and that man would die if he attempted to do such a thing. However, once Bannister had broken through that physical and mental barrier, other runners successfully achieved a mile distance in under four minutes.

Remember that there will always be naysayers, and as long as you keep an eye on your goal and your vision and not get side tracked by the negative words of others, then there is no reason you cannot realise your vision.

'The person who says it cannot be done should not interrupt the person doing it.'

~ Ancient Chinese Proverb

Highly successful people say *yes* to the right opportunity when it presents itself. We take risks. We step out of our comfort zone and refuse to let fear prevent us from moving forward. This is a key trait that successful people possess: that ability to say *yes* instead of *no* when opportunity knocks. However, this doesn't authorise you to become a yes person! What I am talking about is the ability to say *yes* to the **right opportunity for you.**

Here are a few examples of opportunities that may present themselves. Think what your immediate response to each one individually might be, then perhaps go back and ask yourself the question *'If I was asked to do this, would I say yes?'* You may find that you have already done some of these or are currently involved in one. Good for you. Now expand that and consider what you have not yet said *yes* to from this list.

1. Join a group or social event that requires you to go alone
2. Join a dating site if single

3. Accept a new job offer
4. Do something that involves a level of risk
5. Move to a different part of the country, or a different country for a job or to be with someone
6. Let others see or hear your talent, or share your talent
7. Travel somewhere, go on an adventure or take a holiday alone
8. Take up a new sport or hobby
9. Do a parachute jump or similar extreme challenge, perhaps for charity
10. Start a new business
11. Re-train to do something you have always wanted to but there was never the right time
12. Write that book/play
13. Go on that date
14. Go for promotion or change your job
15. Be a leader or a coach
16. Volunteer in a field you are compassionate about
17. Make new friends – join networking groups/ attend events/participate in forums/ take classes or join others in a hobby or sport

These are just some examples I could think of that may cause you to ponder a *yes/no* or *what if...* response. There are many other scenarios, challenges and opportunities not on this list. Change is not easy and starting afresh can be very difficult and uncomfortable. However, if you are stuck, lost or simply wanting to find your way in life, then be prepared to accept that opportunity does and will knock. If your usual response may have been a *no* previously, then how about mixing it up with the odd '*Hell Yes!*' Try it! What have you got to lose?

Common sense prevails of course, so don't be fooled into thinking this particular trait is about taking crazy, life threatening risks. That isn't the point I am making. I am talking about not letting fear hold you back from going for new opportunities and challenges. As we have discussed, there are so many types of fear and in saying *yes* to opportunity, there are certain fears to acknowledge and stand up to - fear of the unknown, fear of failing and fear of succeeding, to name just a few. Perhaps it is time to kick fear up the butt and step out and try something new and different in your life.

But What If...?

As we discussed in an earlier chapter, the *what ifs* can be debilitating in allowing you to move forward with goals, dreams, and plans. I speak from experience when I say that placing *what if* when presented with a new opportunity usually has the effect of preventing us from taking a chance on a new direction, relationship or experience. Let's face it, everything could go wrong. We may fail in our business, you may not make the grade, or pass that test and we may make a complete ass of ourselves on our first attempt! So what? How will you know if that will be your outcome if you don't try?

'Opportunity is missed by most people because it is dressed in overalls and looks like work.'
~ Thomas Edison, Inventor

Let's take a look at Thomas Edison, the inventor of the lightbulb. In attempting to succeed in this quest to invent it, he had 1,000 unsuccessful attempts. Were these failures? No. They were simply steps towards achieving his goal. What if he had given up after the first, second or 999th unsuccessful attempt? Hands up...how many of us would have given up way before the 50th attempt, even? Oh and if you weren't aware, he also invented the phonograph, the Dictaphone, the electric lamp and the automatic printer, to name but a few. And if you think it was okay for him because he was super intelligent, note that his teachers called him stupid and he was fired from his first two jobs!

Did Thomas Edison listen to those naysayers or adopt the 'stupid' label? No he didn't. He believed in himself and his ideas. The guy never gave up!!!

Say Yes

There are so many reasons to say *no,* so why not say **yes** for a change? The benefits to saying a big, fat resounding 'YES!' are more than you could imagine right now in your present situation. The great civil rights leader Martin Luther King Jr. famously stated,

> *'Take the first step in faith. You don't have to see the whole staircase. Just take the first step.'*

Firstly, by saying *yes*, you are letting in more opportunity to have fun. You are creating for yourself a more optimal life. By taking on a new challenge, whether it's a new job, a hobby, an event, a relationship or any other opportunity, you are allowing the new into your life. And the new could be fun!

Secondly, think of the exciting new options that saying *yes* could bring into your life. If you are single and you take up a new hobby, join a gym or even join a dating site, you may be opening yourself up to love. Yes... *love* or at least a chance of a short romance, or even finding new friends. How could it happen if you keep say *no*? I have two really good male friends from being on dating sites and I had a great love experience that was very healing for me, despite ending in a bruised heart. It was a crucial experience I had to go through to learn lessons and develop into the person I now am. I had to know what heartache felt like so I could relate to others going through it, including those close to me. I also received some important advice from this man that I will always carry with me. If I hadn't been on that particular dating site suggested by a friend, I would not have met him.

Joining that site was a huge risk for me. It's a site that relies on existing members voting in new members based on their physical appearance. It's an awful idea in retrospect, but my friend assured me I should try it as she met her partner on there. You have to be deemed 'beautiful enough' and at that time, I was so stuck in fear and strangled by lack of confidence, poor self-esteem and a low regard for my physical appearance, that I honestly believed I was far from beautiful. It also takes 48 hours to be voted in and you can see the voting structure. Many voted against me and for those 48 hours I wanted to quit many times because I was sure I wasn't going to be voted in. It's such a vain and egotistical process, which I would never repeat again. However, I got in and I met that guy. He was the only guy I dated from the site and at the time, I truly believed he was 'the one'.

I could have said *no* and I could have listened to my doubts and negative self-talk, but I stuck with the *yes*. That experience played a significant role in my self-development process and of course for re-building my confidence after divorce.

You may have experienced a significant life-changing situation, such as recovering from serious illness, or the death of a friend or loved one. Perhaps an opportunity has arisen where *saying yes* to a fundraising event, for example, might benefit a charity that is close to your heart and thus might help with the healing process. There may be benefits towards your healing from the suffering and heartache you are experiencing due to your experience or loss. *Saying yes* could enable you to meet people in similar situations or who share the same experiences.

I have a friend who joined a parents' forum related to her son's extreme physical challenges, some of which are life limiting. By doing so, she opened the door to a support network and new friendships. She told me that she finally felt like she fit in somewhere where others understood her and knew what challenges she faced. She said that when she walked into the meeting room for the first time at a parents' weekend conference organised by the charity, she felt like she had 'walked into a room of people just like her'. She no longer felt as isolated as she had been previously feeling.

Recently, I began to do live readings of my poems on a social media platform. I'd started posting my poems on my page a couple of months ago when work slowed down. Though I had been writing these rhyming poem odes for my friends and family for many years, I had kept them hidden from the world. Then, encouraged by a friend, I started to share them on an open mic at her local quarterly poetry event about fifteen months ago.

To say I was nervous at getting up to perform my poetry at my first open mic event was an understatement. I had sweaty hands, washing machine tummy, dry throat and the desire to run out that door quicker than my mate could down a pint! But I made a promise to my friend (not the same one as the beer guzzler) and to myself that I would do it. I said yes when asked. So despite my nerves, I got up and though my delivery wasn't the best, I performed my poem. Subsequently I did open mic many more times at her events, before the virus caused social lockdown. Truthfully, I was always nervous at standing up there with around 50-80 people watching, but I got up each time and did it. During these open mics, I may have had decent enough poems, but my delivery left much room for improvement.

A couple of weeks ago, two of my friends suggested I read my poems out live on a social media platform whilst in lockdown and isolated at home. They assured me I was capable and that I had a receptive audience. I wasn't sure. I still had the *'what if...'* question in my head. Then a colleague from a media networking group I had recently joined requested that I read some of my poems on their forum for their podcast. He had read the poems I'd been submitting onto my social media page and decided I was good enough. Despite my lack of confidence in my delivery, I said *yes*!

Last week I went live for the first time and out of my mouth, unrehearsed, came the words 'I am setting a challenge. Comment a word or phrase and I will write you a poem and recite it on here.' I had six contributions. Since then I regularly recite live poetry and also post my recorded poetry readings. Next week my first poetry book will be out on Amazon and I have already sold almost fifty pre-ordered copies to friends and supporters.

Where will all this lead? Right now I am not sure. I cannot work as the country is in lockdown and my work in both events and make up artistry has temporarily ended. I have no current income. So I am writing and reciting. I have created a new avenue for my life but am still unsure of the direction or the end result. What I do know, however, is that if I did not say *yes* to my friend all those months back, then this new path would not have opened itself up to me.

~~~~~~~~~~

Saying **yes** has so many more benefits than you may see at the outset. Many more options and opportunities may present themselves to you because you decided to step out of your comfort zone and say **YES**!

'Opportunities don't just happen, you create them.'
~ Ancient Chinese Proverb

So let's take a look at five scenarios that saying *yes* to opportunity might bring into your life. These are simply examples, but try to visualise yourself as the person saying *yes*. Pick a scenario that suits you and visualise yourself *saying yes.*

EXERCISE 9: SAYING YES EXAMPLES

1. Offered a New Job in a New Company

Imagine this scenario: You aren't happy in your current job, or are being bullied, or cannot get past the ceiling in your current role within the company. It's making you sad, depressed or anxious, and you feel trapped. Then someone tells you about a job they saw advertised in their company. It's an amazing opportunity and it's a company where you have always wanted to work. Plus the salary on offer is more money than you have ever earned before. However, it's a more demanding role and it will require you to learn new skills, be more visible to others, or to travel.

How do you react? What are your initial thoughts or emotions? Do you react with fear or trepidation? Are you worried about whether you are good enough or qualified enough to apply for the post? Do you fear change from your known job to this new role? Or perhaps you fear rejection by applying for the job and thinking you won't be offered an interview or progress past the interview process? Then what about your thoughts on your current employer? Do you worry that they might not give you a good reference, or that you will be leaving friendships you have built within the team, department or company? What are your initial thoughts and what are your emotions?

Imagine this end result – you went for the interview. It was a great interview and you felt you connected and communicated yourself well to the interviewer. You left the room feeling uplifted and excited for the first time in ages. You have hope. You were invited to a second interview. Again you did well. Then you receive a letter in the post. It's an offer for the job. In fact, they liked you so much, that they are increasing the salary, outlined you for future promotion and are offering you a week's external training course before the job begins. You hand in your notice at your current company and they give you a glowing reference. They then throw you a leaving party and your work colleagues are delighted for you and promise to remain in touch.

Now how do you feel? Better? Uplifted? Experience those happy emotions: it could be you!

2. Going on a Date

You've been single for a while. Your marriage/relationship ended a while ago. You have been focused on bringing up the children and/or working and have had no time or inclination to find someone else. You may have lost confidence in your appearance or are nervous about the dating process and meeting someone new. Your fear of taking this step is holding you back and you worry that you may never meet anyone again.

Then a friend suggests you join a dating site, or to join them on a double date, or perhaps want to introduce you to a single friend of theirs. How do you feel? What are your initial thoughts? Do you punch the air with joy or run behind the sofa to hide? Does your stomach twist in knots of anxiety as you look in your wardrobe for something to wear? Do you worry about your appearance or your ability to hold a conversation? If it's been a long time since you dated someone, and you may have many negative emotions kicking around, as well as many doubts and self-questioning moments.

Imagine this end result – you say yes and agree to go on the date. You get there a few minutes late and he is at the bar waiting. He smiles at you and goes in to kiss your cheek. Your eyes lock in mutual appreciation. He offers to buy you a drink and you spend the next two hours with someone you felt like you have known your entire life. He kisses you on the cheek when it's time to leave, but not before you have arranged a second date. This time at a favourite restaurant you both enjoy. You go home with a huge smile on your face.

How do you feel? What are your emotions?

4. Start a New Sideline Business

You've been offered a business opportunity with low startup costs that you can do from home alongside your job, or whilst at home bringing up the kids. The company has a proven track record and you know people who are already in this or a similar type of business; some are making a great income and seem very happy and successful.

Yet you have so many doubts. What If it doesn't work for you? What if you spend much needed money and it fails? What if you can't make sales, or grow a team or get support from family or friends? What if you don't have the time for it, or start it and then can't give it the time it requires? Have you noticed how many *'what if...?'* questions arise when presented with this type of challenge or opportunity? Having previously run an online business for over four years, I heard every doubt and *what if* imaginable. Running an online business may not be for everyone and not everybody is going to make a fortune doing it, but the secondary opportunities that could arise out of saying yes to starting an online business are worth it.

I may not have reached top levels or achieved the financial success I hoped I would, but the knowledge and self-confidence I gained because of it are one of the reasons I am able to write this book today. I gained so much insight into myself from doing the self-development work that this opportunity encourages, as well as added confidence and self-belief that I did not possess before. I would recommend this type of business to anyone wanting to have more social engagement, build self-confidence and self-esteem and have the chance to earn extra income and awards. My advice, however, is to do your research and ask lots of questions before signing up to anything that requires a financial commitment.

Imagine the end result – you are running your online business and received your first promotion and earned yourself the title 'Star of the Month'. You haven't received an award like that since you were in school! You also earned yourself a financial bonus and a huge bouquet of flowers. For the first time in many years, you are being shown appreciation for something you have achieved. You see a bright future for yourself and your children and your dreams are getting bigger and bolder for the first time in a long time.

How are you feeling? What are your emotions?

These three scenarios are simple examples of opportunities that may be offered that you could either say yes or no to. The idea is to open your mind to the possibilities. Not every new situation or opportunity is going to match your requirements or sit right with you, but if your immediate response is *what if*, then ask yourself what your concerns are and if there are fears stopping your from taking that leap into the unknown.

'The bravest are surely those who have the clearest vision of what is before them, glory and danger alike, and yet withstanding, go out and meet it,'
~ Thucydides, Ancient Philosopher

EXERCISE 9 (BONUS): TRY THESE SCENARIOS FOR YOURSELF

Try these following scenarios as you did for the above. Firstly, do the fear/doubt/what if feelings and emotions associated with the opportunity. Then write down your emotions for how you might feel having successfully completed the event. Use the space below for notes, or use your notebook or a sheet of paper to conduct this exercise. Have fun with it!

- Do a presentation
- Do a live video for your business or to give a message
- Attend or contribute to an event
- Travel for work/business
- Start a new hobby
- Take action on a suggestion to enhance your business
- Spend more time with your children

WHAT IF...   I SAID YES   I FEEL...

When Saying No is a Positive

One of the traits of being highly successful is knowing when to say *yes* and when to say *no*. Nobody deserves to be anyone else's doormat, or to be so compliant that one becomes a 'yes man'. There are times when saying *no* is essential for strength of character and for self-empowerment. So when is it okay to say *no* as opposed to *yes*?

A successful person knows when to delegate. Sometimes saying *yes* to more work and responsibility can make us less efficient and even take us further from our goals. Therefore it is positive to say *no* to things that are creating a distraction from being effective in the process of attaining our goals.

Highly successful people have learned the benefits of saying *no*. It can be very empowering and give back more control over your life.

There are so many distractions in our lives, from television, to mobile phones and technology, clutter, background noise, messaging and emails, conversations and meetings, to name but a few. When we overcommit or multi task, it takes away focus from the thing, vision or goal. Sometimes it is essential to say no to remain focused on the task. If you spend your evenings watching television for hours, then that is a huge distraction to achieving your goals. Saying *no* can help us create more focus in our lives. That, in turn, allows us to see the *yes* opportunity when it arrives.

Sometimes when we are saying *yes* to others we are often saying *no* to ourselves and that may not be the best answer for our wellbeing and the pursuit of our vision. So saying *no* can establish healthy boundaries with others and also improve your own opportunities because it frees us up to be more accessible when an opportunity arises. It also enables us to contemplate what is best for us as opposed to what it best for others; thus creating space to put ourselves first for a change. It can also help to build deeper and stronger friendships, because we have built stronger boundaries, and therefore others may respect us more.

This reminds me of the scene in one of my favourite Rom Com films, '27 Dresses'. The main character Jane (actress Katherine Heigl) is being told by love interest Kevin (actor James Marsden) that she doesn't say *no* enough. He teaches her to start saying *no*, something that she struggles to do. She is the epitome of a 'yes girl' and it often leaves her unhappy, unfulfilled and dis-empowered. Learning to say *no* was the start of her enlightenment and empowerment. And if you want to know what happens at the end there is no spoiler here – go watch the film!

So, if you find you are a *yes* person, maybe it's time to take stock of why and re-evaluate what you really want. Final words on this are taken from a quote I read in a magazine:

'You have to learn to say no without feeling guilty. Setting boundaries is healthy. You need to learn to respect and take care of yourself.'

~ Author Unknown

Regret

'Dead people receive more flowers than living people, because regret is stronger than gratitude.'
~ Anne Frank, The Diary of Anne Frank

How powerful is that quote from Anne Frank's diary? What insight this young girl had because of the challenges that faced her and her family whilst hiding from the Nazi persecution of Jews in the Netherlands. This is a child who lived in fear of being captured, yet still wrote of hope, love and not having regrets.

Regret is a powerful emotion.

It's such a debilitating and negative emotion to feel. If saying *yes* to an opportunity and experiencing the positive effects creates elated emotions, imagine the emotions regret conjures. We have all experienced regret in some form or another in our lives.

There are many reasons to suffer regret and many emotions arise because of it - anger, worry, lack of accomplishment and feelings of failure, remorse and sorrow. The opportunities we miss that create a feeling of regret and the stain regret leaves on us can feel like a permanent mark.

I have a few regrets myself. This is one of my most painful personal regret stories, and if I think too long and hard about it, then it can still tear me down in tears.

I was at work in London and it was a Tuesday. Two days previous, I had visited my terminally ill mother in Wales for her sixtieth birthday. Saying goodbye that Sunday was an awful experience. I knew she had merely weeks left to live.

She wasn't emotional as she was always such a strong woman who rarely gave hugs or expressed loving emotions. That wasn't to say she didn't love me, but rather she struggled to express feelings of deep love. She was trying to give me personal things of hers without her husband, my stepfather at that time, noticing. He was an alcoholic tyrant who over the years had done his best to isolate her emotionally from her children.

However, the way she was trying to gift me her jewellery was so awkward, that I couldn't accept. 'Take something from the (jewellery) cupboard.' She gestured with her bony hand. If she had taken some item out and presented it to me then I may have graciously accepted it, but this felt too much like thieving from her. I simply couldn't.

I walked away with her sewing machine. She was a seamstress and her sewing machines were precious to her. Ironically, I never used it, as at first it was too painful to make use of and then it accidentally got broken in our many house moves later down the line. I didn't want to take it, or anything else, but she insisted. I guess I didn't want such a final acknowledgment of her impeding passing.

I called her around eleven am two days later, from my desk at work. It was a glorious, hot June summer morning. She was in a perky mood on the phone and we discussed how to make protein shakes and thick soups to help give her energy and perhaps add more weight to her. At this stage she was merely skin and bone and hanging onto life by sinewy threads of hope and fear.

I told her I was going to book two weeks annual leave later that afternoon to spend some quality time with her. We planned what we would do and got ourselves excited over merely being together. I should have spent more time with her before that, but I was so busy with life and work and her husband made it so difficult to visit. So this was a chance to make amends and to spend great decent time with the mother I adored before she left me.

Less than two hours later I received a call at work. It was from my older sister. My mum had a stroke and she was probably not going to make the morning. She told me to get up there now.

My boss was great and I left immediately. I went home to pack. I didn't know how long I would be there. Yet my husband asked me to wait until the plumber left our house so he could drive me there. He wanted to be with me. We were having a kitchen installed. I waited and waited. Hours ticked by and I was a state. Finally, five hours after the phone call, we left for the four hour drive up to Wales. By the time I finally arrived at my mother's house, I was too late. She had passed twenty minutes before we got there and despite being the first person my sister called, I was the last person to arrive.

The grief was unbearable, but the pain of regret at not being with her when she passed as everyone else had been, was even more crushing than the loss of her. For many years I held that against my husband. He was sorry too, but for many years, in my heart I couldn't let him off the hook. It was many years later, after our marriage ended and I started working on myself, that I realised, the person I truly needed to forgive was myself. I chose to wait for him; I chose not to jump on a train or take the coach. I chose not to grab the car and undertake the longest journey I had driven to date and face my fear of driving over the Severn Bridge (a huge fear for me at that time). Instead, I waited and waited and gave my power over to someone else. That was my biggest regret: that I didn't make the right choice for me or for someone I loved.

'A man with outward courage dares to die, a man with inner courage dares to live.'
~ Lao Tzu, Ancient Philosopher

Sometimes life doesn't work out for us and we literally cannot see the wood from the trees. We make mistakes and beat ourselves up for not taking that opportunity or going for that job interview, date, trip of a lifetime. Those times happen to all of us. The important point is that we do not stay in that space; we let go of regret and move forward. Throughout this book I have quoted many ancient Chinese proverbs and ancient philosophers. That is because I connect with their wisdom; a wisdom that has survived hundreds of years, if not centuries, and is as relevant today as it was then. This proverb I adore. It's so profound and covers loss as well as regret:

'You cannot prevent the birds of sorrow from flying over your head, but you can prevent them from building nests in your hair.'

So, if someone offers you an opportunity, whatever that opportunity is and your immediate reaction may be to say *no*, take a moment and think, *What if I say yes? What's the worst thing that could happen?* If it isn't going to make you someone's doormat, or place you in unnecessary danger, then what the heck have you got to lose? Life is way too short for regrets...

"In the end, we only regret the chances we didn't take, relationships we were afraid to have, and the decisions we were afraid to make.'

~ Author Unknown

EXERCISE 10: REGRET LIST

1. Create a list of things you regret. This may be things you never did, opportunities you didn't take, situations you would do differently if given the opportunity again, or things you regret you said or did. This may be painful to do, so come back to this when you are ready, or visit and re-visit and add to the list.

* Note – although I have left space below, try to write these regrets on a separate sheet of paper. Use the space below to scribble notes, quotes, regrets etc. in pencil if possible.

2. When you are confident with your list, then get rid of it. That's right, dispose of that damn thing! Those are all 'gone' situations and your future has no place for regrets. Either screw up the list and chuck it in the bin, or safely burn it.

It is time to move on with your life and your life has no room for regrets!!

LIST OF REGRETS

Chapter Summary

1. If someone offers you an opportunity don't immediately say 'no'. Stop. Breathe and think first. Can you change it to a 'yes' answer?
2. Know when opportunity is knocking.
3. Ignore the *what ifs.*
4. Say yes and figure out the how later.
5. Saying yes to one opportunity could open the door to another.
6. Do not be a yes person. It's also fine to say no!
7. Make a list of things you would like to do but never had the courage to.
8. Recognise the power of regret.
9. Most people regret the things they didn't do more than the things they did. What do you regret that you cannot change?
10. Make a list of past regrets and let them go. Let go of the past and welcome in new opportunities for the future.

Case Study 12 – Philip on Saying Yes to Opportunity

I was a skinny, shy boy lacking in confidence at school. Academically, I was a poor performing pupil.

My science teacher took pity on me and helped me with extra lessons after school with a few other pupils.

He also invited me to join his after school badminton club.

I had never held a badminton racket before and declined his offer at first, because I was not a 'sporty' and was concerned I may make a fool of myself.

However, my teacher eventually said, "What have you got to lose?"

Eventually I took the plunge - very nervously at first.

To my surprise, I took to it like a duck to water and was enjoying it. Within a few months I got into the school's badminton team and become Captain of the team!

Saying 'YES' to <u>this </u>opportunity started a chain of events, which when I look back is a miracle. It transformed a skinny kid into a sporty person.

I went on to compete at a very high level in this sport and with this newly found confidence, started to work out and developed quite a good physique.

This started a domino effect and the confidence to participate in other sports. Eventually I was achieving County and National standards and beyond in over half a dozen sports, winning titles, trophies and medals, etc.

After retiring from competition, I turned to coaching and

over time, a number of my trainees eventually competed at County, National, World and Olympics, winning medals in gymnastics, trampolining, athletics, fencing, canoeing, table tennis, badminton, swimming, basketball, hockey, shooting, archery, etc., whilst others went on to professional sporting careers like football, cricket and ballet!

Saying 'YES' to a simple opportunity to do something that I had never done before transformed my life and the lives of others over a period of over 50 years.

The ripple effect down the road has been amazing in my personal achievement, as well as the opportunity to have trained thousands of people in the joy of participating and competing in sports.

YOUR ATTITUDE IN ONE AREA PERMEATES THROUGHOUT EVERY OTHER AREAS OF YOUR LIFE!

Remember, at school I was also a 'failed' academic student and was in the bottom three kids in the bottom set!

Mr Roland Duff, my maths teacher, made the most profound difference in my life.

He said two things to me that blew my mind.

He said, "If you honestly don't understand something – ASK!"

Secondly, "It is better to FEEL STUPID for 5 minutes then STAY STUPID for the rest of your life."

WOW!

As a result of saying 'YES' to his offer of help and being prepared to ask for help, within two terms, I managed to get to set 2 in most subjects and one of the only six pupils to take Advanced Level Mathematics and become a teacher.

Today, I am known as the global 10 Seconds Maths Expert!

~ Philip Chan, Entrepreneur, Coach, Teacher, Mentor, Ten Seconds Maths Genius, Bodyguard.

CHAPTER 7

TRAIT 6: **BE A DISRUPTOR**

'A person or thing that prevents something, especially a system, process or event, from continuing as usual or as expected.'

~ Cambridge English Dictionary Description of a Disruptor

I once had a boyfriend who described himself as a 'disruptor'. I hadn't a clue what that meant at the time. I assumed it to be a business thing, and since I wasn't involved in his line of international high-end, commercial business environment, then I dismissed it merely as an attribute I should work on acquiring for myself.

Four years later, the world is facing its biggest challenge. The Covid-19 virus has created a global pandemic with catastrophic effects on almost every business and certainly every individual. Not only have we suddenly had our freedom compromised, but the infrastructure of the global economy, financial markets and day-to-day life as we knew it merely weeks ago, has been impacted in such a way that life may never be the same again for the majority of people on this planet. Now that is some major disruption!

As yet, since we are in the throes of this pandemic, nobody

knows what the true outcome will be, or even precisely how or where the virus originated from. There are so many conspiracy theories kicking around, including thoughts on this originating from a select group of people. As the saying goes, 'time will tell'.

Right now, globally, humanity is facing some of the greatest challenges to our survival and existence. Our response is crucial for where we go from here, both individually and collectively. So how do we respond? How you respond to any significant challenge is key to your growth and your growth mindset. Let's take a look at what that means.

Growth Mindset vs Fixed Mindset

According to research conducted by author and Stanford Professor Carol Dwek, our thinking can fall into two types of mindset: growth mindset or fixed mindset. Take a look at the defining factors below of both types of mindset, then consider which camp you sit in right now.

Growth Mindset

Sees risks as a chance to improve and innovate change

Sees failure as a chance to learn

Sees criticism as a chance to improve

Embraces challenging tasks and works hard to improve and expand

Holds a belief in personal growth and expansion

Believes you are in control of your abilities

Believes skills are built

You can persevere no matter your age or obstacles

Obstacles are an opportunity for problem solving and experimenting

When frustrated, believes in perseverance

Doesn't quit

Fixed Mindset

Takes fewer risks

Failure is permanent

Takes criticism personally

Takes the easy path and puts in minimal effort

Doesn't like to be challenged

Believes you cannot learn and grow

Abilities determine everything and accomplishments are measurable

You are born with skills and intelligence and these are set

Threatened by the success of others

Gives up easily when frustrated

Quits easily

Why even try

We are innate and unchangeable

Where do you sit? What is your mindset bias? Whilst it's true that most of us will not comfortably fit into either camp without carrying at least one of these traits from an opposite mindset to the one we feel more inclined to, we will tend to favour one type of mindset over the other in our beliefs.

Before I began a journey of growth and self-development, I know I possessed more than a few of the *fixed* mindset traits. I wanted to quit often, gave up easily, took criticism to heart, didn't like to be challenged, wanted to give up when obstacles or frustration blocked me, and allowed my abilities and achievements to determine how successful I saw myself. I sat firmly in the *fixed* mindset camp.

Look where I am now. Using small steps to begin with, I started to move camps. I began to change the way I looked at things and suddenly my world began to change around me. I began to adopt a *growth* mindset. Today, I have two feet firmly planted in that camp, because I allowed my mindset to adapt to new possibilities and thus embrace positive changes in my life. It wasn't easy at first to switch teams, but necessary. If you find yourself with more characteristics in the *fixed* mindset camp, then begin with the words *I can* and take baby steps from there.

Having a *growth* mindset allows you to grow, learn and achieve more over time. It also enables you to think outside of the box and adopt the characteristic traits of a disruptor.

What Is A Disruptor?

According to Dictionary.com, the definition of a disruptor is '*to destroy, usually temporarily, the normal continuance or unity of... to cause disorder or turmoil...*'

A person who is called a disruptor will usually be described as such within a business setting. There are entire companies that fall in the category of a 'Disruptor Company' – Apple, Uber, Spotify, Peloton, Amazon, Netflix and Airbnb are just some recent examples of companies that have disruption at the core of their advancement. Let's take a brief look at three of these companies to see how the changes they implemented affected how their markets then changed.

Netflix, founded in 1998, took the concept of consumers' home renting films to another level. Instead of going into a shop to rent a film or having one delivered to your door, Netflix came up with the idea of streaming. A film could be streamed into your home directly. Then in 2013, it went on to establish itself as a producer of high quality content with its release of 'House of Cards.'

Airbnb, founded in 2008, revolutionised the way we think about accommodation in the travel industry. The idea of paid home sharing became a new concept and as such, the market followed suit with the birth of similar companies with similar concepts.

Peloton, founded in 2012, introduced daily, live streaming spinning classes into consumers' homes. They currently offer approximately 4,000 on-demand studio experience classes and 14 daily spinning classes, with next generation indoor bikes (purchased by the consumer), for a monthly subscription.

~~~~~~~~~~

Whilst many of us are not going to be headhunted by one of the world's top companies with the mission of disrupting the status quo and developing innovative new ideas to blow the competition out of the water, we can impact our own lives and businesses by adopting a disruptive mindset.

Firstly, let's take a look at the characteristics I suggest you learn to adopt if you want to have a disruptor approach to your life.

Characteristics of a Disruptor

- They are innovative
- They never get comfortable
- They view life through a different lens to others
- They continue to improve themselves
- They are brave and they take risks
- They get out of their comfort zone
- They think and act differently
- They can create chaos to achieve results
- They recognise opportunity
- They trust their gut instinct
- They have an eye on the future
- They trust themselves
- They always questions their own preconceptions about things
- They ignore the critics and the naysayers
- They stand up for themselves
- They are prepared to have a voice
- They question how things are done
- They want change, lead change and take charge
- They ask for what they want
- They can destabilise the status quo
- They think outside of the box
- They have a vivid imagination
- They have obsessive focus
- They have a deep curiosity about the world and business
- They are willing to try something new
- They follow their passion
- They look for the unmet need and fresh ideas
- They are willing to re-invent themselves
- They are adaptable and flexible
- They want to learn new skills
- They are ambitious and focused on high growth
- They reject old paradigms
- They are trailblazers
- They stay ahead of the game
- They have passion, tenacity and vision

These are just some of the personal characteristics of a disruptor. Notice that many of them coincide with the characteristics of having a *growth* mindset?

So what do you need to do to adopt a more disruptive attitude to life? Firstly, check whether your mindset is on the growth side as opposed to the fixed. If not, then try working on changing your thinking to adopt a *growth* mindset. Then, start saying *yes* a heck of a lot more often than you may be doing now.

If you want to learn more about being a disruptor and perhaps introducing more of these attributes to your personal life or business, I suggest researching books such as 'Disrupt Yourself: Putting the Power of Disruptive Innovation to Work' by author Witney Johnson and 'Disruptors: Success Strategies from Women Who Break The Mold' by Dr Patti Fletcher.

Apart from adopting some of the characteristics listed above, there are other changes you could make that will help you to move forward with your life. Who do you surround yourself with? Look at the people closest to you and those in your social network. Do they have a growth mindset? Are they wanting to better themselves or move forward with their lives? Will they support and encourage you to make changes to your own life, to be successful, to help you to fulfil your dreams and help you chase bigger goals?

Perhaps it may be worth investing in a coach or personal mentor to help get you to where you want to go. I may have eventually ended up where I am now, but having a life coach on board in the form of Richard Marchand helped me get there a heck of a lot sooner!

'A single conversation with a wise man is worth a month's study of books.'
~ Ancient Chinese Proverb

When you disrupt yourself, you give courage to those around you to be courageous and to want to change or improve their lives. A disruptive idea is contagious and can have an impact on others. Not only can it positively make an impact on yourself, but also on those around you. Emotions are contagious; when you feel good or happy, others around you feed off those emotions.

Become a Self-Disruptor

If you are in a stuck place and want to move to an unstuck place, then you can become a self-disruptor. Making a decision to become someone you are currently not or to do something you currently aren't doing involves making a decision to try something new. When you are learning new things and becoming creative, you start to feel good about yourself. This in turn releases dopamine into our brain and that neurotransmitter makes us feel great, happy and cheerful. This in turn affects those around us, because by feeling happy, the hormone oxytocin is released from the posterior lobe of our pituitary gland. This hormone is nicknamed the 'cuddle hormone' or the 'love hormone' because oxytocin is released when we cuddle, bond or share love with others. When we feel happy, we release happy vibes to those around us.

So go try something new and create!

'The act of creation is singular, as is the moment of creation, and the result of something fresh and strange.'

~ Peter Thiel, Founder of PayPal

If you want to get ahead in your business or want to start up a business, then ask yourself if you can adopt some of the disruptive attributes aforementioned to look at new ways to give yourself an advantage over your colleagues or players in the current market. Do it better than what already exists and become a game changer. A disruptive idea is very powerful.

'Disruption isn't just doing things in a different way that doesn't resonate or go any further or becomes a one off, because that's more of a gimmick. Being disruptive is about changing the game.'

~ James Kirkham, Chief Strategy Officer of Football Connect Creator Copa90

One of my favourite lines is from a film called 'Robots', one of my kids' animation films. The main character is a robot called Rodney who, despite his own lowly circumstances, offers to fix the other robots' broken parts. As he gets out his tools he declares with determination, *'See a need, fill a need'.*

There will always be a need and a disruptive person may be the one who sees the need first, especially in a business sense. It takes time and determination and patience to get to where you may want to go, but why wait to start? Take note of this Chinese proverb and just start!

'A journey of a thousand miles begins with a single step.'

So what are you waiting for? Do something amazing, astonishing and unexpected and make positive, determined steps towards achieving your goals. Go disrupt yourself, and if you are fearful of change or disrupting your life, remember these wonderful words from Albert Einstein,

'Insanity is doing the same thing over and over again and expecting different results.'

Take Action

'Knowledge, if it does not determine action, is dead to us.'

~ Plotinus, Ancient Philosopher

So you've figured out who you are, recognised and taken stock of your fears, written down your goals, created a vision board and have been doing visualisation, affirmations and meditation until what you want has been drummed into your subconscious mind.

You've looked at your regrets and let go of all that has been holding you back. Or at least you intend to. Yes, now you have intention and you recognise that in order for your life to change, your thoughts and self-talk has to change also. Then you've learned about the power of saying yes and when it's ok to say no! You've probably recognised that it's about time you rocked your world with changes and disrupted your own life. You are ready to take new steps towards a brand new you. Now what?

Now you TAKE ACTION!

'Your teacher can open the door, but you must enter by yourself.'

~ Ancient Chinese Proverb

For many people, the hardest step to take is the first one. When I decided I wanted to write a book, I was a teenager. In fact, I had the crazy notion of one of my books becoming a film one day. Crazy because I didn't come from a world where those dreams were anyone's reality. I didn't live in a film or media environment, or even go to the cinema that often. I just had this inner vision of that actually transpiring in my life one day. This was definitely a crazy, reach for the moon, C type goal. Yesterday, I got a contract for my first poetry book to be published. This book I am writing is almost complete. I started seven months ago. I wrote half in eight weeks, but then put it aside until four weeks ago. And now you are reading it.

The point is that I had a dream when I was fifteen. At twenty-five, I wrote a full novel and submitted it to twenty plus publishers unsolicited. Unfortunately, it was rejected by all of them. Many of the publishers took the time to write beautiful and encouraging notes with the rejection letters. However, I only saw the rejection and not the encouragement. I put the book aside (currently sitting in a box in my garage) and only put pen to paper again eight years ago. The point is that I took action on my dream and although the dream is only now starting to be realised, I saw myself as a published writer as a child.

Yes, sometimes life kicks us in the teeth. Sometimes we get thrown so many lemons that we are floored and bruised and not in the right headspace to reply with a jug of lemonade! However, if you have a goal, no matter how big or small, each step you take towards it is a step closer to you achieving that goal. Remember that saying '*A journey of a thousand miles begins with one step*' (Lao Tzu)? It's time to take that one step. It's time to do the thing, or those things you need to do in order to get to where you want to go. It's time to stop acting small and step into your true power. Going back to the wisdom of Rumi,

'*Stop acting so small. You are the Universe in static motion.*'

It's as simple as that. Take the first step. For example, if you decided you wanted to retrain to become a counsellor or therapist, would you declare to your friends and family 'Hey! I'm now a counsellor' if you hadn't first earned the qualification to practise? The initial step would be to make the decision, then find a course, commit to that course and gain the professional qualifications. These are the action steps you embark on to become a qualified counsellor or therapist. Once achieved, you are then ready to announce your newly qualified status and availability to the world.

Sometimes it is hard to take the initial steps. The end goal may seem distant and the path ahead rocky and filled with many challenges, but the most important step to take is the first. Then keep walking, step-by-step, until you are in a position to take stock of where you are and realise that it is further to go back than it is to go forward. Imagine the feeling of achieving the end result. Put yourself on the final step and about to realise your goal. One more step to take forward and it's yours. How does that feel?

Acting 'As If'

Author, teacher and prophet Neville Goddard, who died in 1972, spoke about creating imaginary stories and acting 'as if'. He believed that we are all God and that imagination is the most powerful tool we have to achieve our goals and visions. He devised the concept of 'imagining the wish fulfilled.' To do this, he suggested we ignore our present reality and instead imagine we have fulfilled the end desire. We breathe in that emotion and envision the realisation of the end result. He focused on the emotion of feeling 'the wish fulfilled.' The important part is the imagining of the end result and the emotion you attach to it; the fulfilling of your desires, wishes and goals.

Think back to the advice I offered my friend when she panicked about the awards ceremony and how I suggested she imagine being at the event and receiving her award. Implanting the suggestion into her imagination took away her fears and helped her to visualise a positive result. Coincidentally, she did go on to win that award.

Werner Erhard, author and founder of the Landmark Forum and whom The New York Times once called 'The Father of Self Help', stated, *'Create your future from your future not your past'*. The past is the past. It is time to learn from its lessons and let go, and time to focus on the future that you want for your life.

Once you have your vision, once you *truly* know what it is you want to achieve, it is up to you to go out and take that first step to make it happen. To be successful, you have to be brave enough to take that first step and to take action towards achieving the end result.

One of the biggest impacts on my mind and thought process back in September 2018, when I truly embarked on my life changing journey with life coach Richard Marchand, was a passage I listened to. The great Earl Nightingale, American radio speaker and author, had a spoken passage called The Strangest Secret (1957). I listened to this every day for 30 days. It was an integral part of the process of my mindset change. I would listen to his words of wisdom over and over until they melted into the framework of my subconscious. I recommend everyone reading this book to look it up and listen to this passage. It's old and in black and white, but the message is as profound and relevant today as it was seventy-three years ago. Do the thing and gain that power!

'You were born with wings, why prefer to crawl through life?'

~ Rumi

Chapter Summary

- Adopt a growth mindset
- Adopt characteristics of a disruptor
- Understand the importance of taking action
- Take the first step towards your goals and dreams

Case Study 13: James on Being a Disruptor

THE JOYS OF DISRUPTION
BY JAMES MURPHY

If I say the word 'disruption' or even 'disruptive', it has instantly negative connotations. Quite logically so, in fact. The world is of course on hold at the time of writing this. Things have been disrupted, dramatically and tragically.

Our first experience of the word comes through childhood and school, no doubt. As in, that 'disruptive' behaviour at the back of a class that impairs a lesson's progress. That is completely understandable.

Your first memories of a word, a notion, a concept stay with you and echo down through the years. So, what if I were to tell you that 'disrupt', 'disruptive', and even 'disruption' can be GOOD things, with positive connotation? You'd be shocked and surprised, perhaps.

But the logic is sound and you should embrace it. You WANT to DISRUPT! You NEED to BE a DISRUPTOR! Let's return, for a second to 'that' current crisis. Yes, we are tested and challenged and locked in and shut down like never before. The greatest problem one could imagine in nominal peacetime, with whichever warlike analogies keep us going.

And yet, it is also fair to say that we as a nation, world, as communities and individuals, took the change in our stride. How? Why? Because we had already begun evolving. We were 'disrupted' long ago, in a positive sense, by the rise of technology and wireless communications.

Our means, manner and motives in the deployment of

technology throughout the past two decades prepared us for this current situation. Not in any direct or conscious way (be gone, conspiracy theorists and prophets!). No. It's more that we have evolved, without even knowing it and now is the test, the concrete proof that there is indeed a positive side to disruption.

This was always the way. Television in its 1950s advent disrupted the use of cinemas, putting the medium's very survival on the line until they learned to co-exist. Today, we face an option to stream more content, more widely and ahead of or in alternative to projected release dates.

The desire to visit the cinema is still 'there', though its supremacy as primary platform for a film has changed, is changing, and no doubt may change more as the months progress. One disruption leads to another. But once again, the disruption is simply a synonym for change. And change itself is neither 'good' nor 'bad'. It is what WE make it; it is how YOU respond, via constant permutation and evolution.

That is not to say that transition is painless. Anyone suggesting that is foolish and those who evangelically promote change for change's sake are to be treated with skeptical suspicion. It is possible, nonetheless, to treat challenges as a status quo in the most proactive, productive and thereby positive manner. You can LIVE the change. You can BE the change.

BECOME that which you FEAR and ACCEPT that loss, impermanence and uprooting are there for the TAKING! ENJOY the threat of working through uncertain conditions; turn the upset of an intrusive sound/noise/worry into the driving force that makes YOU push harder, work longer, and do better.

It need not be a case of you devising some revolutionary

device or game changing development in your sector. Indeed, that KIND of pressure is in very real danger of depleting the true cores of success and distinction, clouding language and legitimising obfuscation.

Notice how EVERYONE is now 'CEO' of a company? The fact that they are a sole trader is beside the point. There is a sense that everyone must now be an expert, have status, project an image. That was born from a once 'disruptive' ideal of a knight/lady/another corporate saviour or trouble-shooter in shining armour. But like all trends, it got stale.

The once revolutionary idea became derivative, dull and devalued. It goes hand in hand with the (very English, by the way) belief that one offers only a service/product. The paradigm cannot be shifted, right? WRONG!

How about standing out not by calling yourself CEO of a startup that just...well...started up...but by being the person who BREAKS that mould, who TALKS sense, honesty, probity and CLARITY. And from THAT position of raw and unfettered linguistic novelty...yes, BE the CHANGE. You are THINKING like a CEO!

You would still operate within the established paradigm's parameters but with a readymade USP. This is not because your service or product in itself reinvents the wheel or is the new Facebook/Microsoft/Alphabet/sliced bread (apologies and congratulations if you are/aren't any of those).

There would just be an aura of optimism, dynamism and 'get up and go' about your presentation. Still you. Still knowing your limitations and being respectful of how others expect business to be done. But just injecting that slight spark of innovation; that hint of self-effacing accessibility and utter determination to never give up.

Does it guarantee you a business network or even a job? No. Will it even garner call-backs and clicks? Absolutely and emphatically a big 'no'. Sorry! But it won't hurt your endeavours, either. That sense of being in absolute and total charge of the market around you WILL enable you to project the KIND of image that, by its nature, helps, rather than harms your business or other ambitions.

That same principle applies to anything else in life that is nominally beyond our control or to those sectors whereby we, like most, are observers/participants rather than leading innovators. I cannot make someone love me/fancy me/date me/marry me. But I can be pleasant, accessible, positive and project a glow of fun fused to purpose. I cannot change the weather, hold back or move forward time, stop death, manipulate the stock market and so on.

I can, though, cease being passive and negative: the reactive can meld into the proactive and need not be mutually exclusive. Healthy skepticism yet open mindedness, all in a cycle and balance that by its nature accepts the certainty of uncertainty and looks right back with a dashing smile. Be THAT person!

Before departing, let's return to that starting image. Disruption in a classroom. Sure, it can be negative and even destructive. But just imagine the child who never disrupts. Even the best behaved and brightest of kids are naughty at some point, even if they stand out BY being bad that day because they are otherwise so good.

And the teacher's job, alongside teaching the subject matter, mentoring, pastoral care and marking and planning, is to somehow engender that JOY in improvement: shaping the learner to improve at being a citizen, a student, a grown up. A good teacher is, in fact...you guessed it...a DISRUPTOR. Worth thinking about, no?

GO FORTH AND BE DISRUPTIVE!

~JAMES MURPHY Studied at New College, Oxford and the College of Law. A Qualified Arbitrator, he is currently prepping a PhD, and is a Director at <u>www.urbanhawk.space</u> as well as Editor in Chief at <u>www.movieviral.com</u> .

CHAPTER 8

TRAIT 7: **DON'T QUIT**

'The temptation to quit will be greatest just before you are about to succeed.'

~ Ancient Chinese Proverb

So you have been doing the work on yourself, addressed your fears, recognised your negative behaviour patterns, started to speak and think more positively and made steps towards your goals. Walls are coming down and constricting self-imposed boundaries are loosening. You feel great, positive, present in the now and truly alive for the first time in a long time. Then BAM! You crash. You hit a wall, fall down, receive criticism, or suffer rejection – once, twice, maybe ten times in a row. Challenges arise and keep coming at you and you feel exhausted and exasperated with the effort to keep going. So what do you do? How do you respond?

'All things are difficult before they are easy.'

~ Ancient Chinese Proverb

This is the time that can either make you or break you. Either way is fine because it's all part of the journey, but to break and stay broken and not get up and back on the path is not going to help you realise your dream. And it will make the journey that much longer. Remember motivational speaker Les Brown's message about getting up? If you fall and you land on your back and can look up, well you are more than capable of getting up. Simple. And you keep getting up and getting up again and again, until the time comes when it's less noticeable, less painful and less costly for you to do so.

Remember one of the previous chapters, in which I listed some of the famous, successful people who failed before they succeeded? Those multi-millionaires who were once bankrupt? They fell, they failed, they suffered rejection and faced the vicious tongues of the naysayers. Did they stay down? Did they give up because of a harsh word, comment or write up? No. They got up. They rose up from the belly of defeat or failure and they continued to pursue their passion or goal.

If you are in a place where you want to quit on your dreams because life is so damn hard, then be reassured that this is a normal, natural process on the path to success. EVERY successful person experiences the same emotions, frustrations and desire to get off that road because of the challenges they face. The difference between someone who is a success and a person who remains mediocre, is that the successful person NEVER QUIT!

Be persistent. Do not give up on your dreams, even when you cannot see the fruit of your labour. Remember the story of the bamboo tree? It took five years from planting for the farmer to see the fruits of his labour. Persistently, he committed to watering and tending to the place where he planted the bamboo seed. He did not give up for those five years because he could not see the results of his commitment. Instead he continued with his goal – to nourish, tend and water the ground. He worked on the foundations in order for the growth to occur. He did not give up and was rewarded with a gigantic tree that grew at a tremendous rate in just six weeks! This Scottish Proverb is a reminder of that:

'Don't judge each day by the harvest you reap, but by the seeds you plant.'

There are many reasons we feel like giving up. We will explore them in further detail here, but first, it's important that we take a look at our belief system in order for us to have a greater understanding of why sometimes, when faced with an obstacle, we fall down the cracks and back into obscurity. Our self-belief and our paradigms are like the soil for the seed that we plant to grow. If the soil is rocky, or not rich with the correct nutrients, or lacking water and nourishment, it is very difficult, though not impossible, for the seed to grow.

What is a Paradigm?

In his book 'The Structure of Scientific Revolutions', American philosopher of science Thomas Khun took the idea suggested over a century earlier by European philosophers such as Karl Marx and Emilie Durkheim that we have a framework of concepts, beliefs, ideas, values and habits that form the basis of our reality. These are called *paradigms*. A person's paradigm is how they perceive the world based on their foundation of belief, or framework of thought and behaviour patterns.

Problems arise when a person sets out on a journey to change some of these old patterns of beliefs and values. This is called a 'paradigm shift'. There is a period in the change behaviours where it can be uncomfortable for the person to make the leap from one set of known beliefs and behaviour patterns to another. It is during this process of change that many people feel the desire to give up and to quit. It is a natural part of the change process, but also one to be recognised, acknowledged and then worked on with the tools and techniques of adopting a positive mindset.

It reminds me of the story of The Three Billy Goats Gruff, a 19th Century Norwegian fairy tale children's book. If you aren't familiar with it, let me give you a brief description.

There are three Billy goats on a hill looking down to a beautiful, lush, green pasture on the other side of a bridge. However, under the bridge lives a nasty troll who eats Billy goats and all who threatens to pass along his bridge. To get to the beautiful lush pasture, the goats have to cross the bridge. Therein lies the dilemma and the lesson. The goats know that to cross the bridge they will have to face the troll, but they cannot stay where they are because the pasture they are currently in is dry and unyielding. They have a choice to make - to stay and starve, or to face the danger of crossing the bridge and get to a better place.

How many of us have had to face dilemmas similar to this before in our own lives? Not literally of course, but use the story as a metaphor for situations and challenges we have had to face: to remain where we are, or to go through the process of change to get to a better place. If we keep the metaphor running, how many of us choose to face and conquer the troll, or stay where we are because of our fear based paradigms?

Change is uncomfortable. To create new paradigms, a new

pattern of beliefs, thoughts processes, values and habits, we have to go through this 'paradigm shift'. That is the place where so many people stop, walk away or simply give up.

We all have a set of beliefs in place from childhood and the majority of them were given to us by our parents, school and society. For example, I was told by a good friend at sixteen that I couldn't sing and this was reinforced by my ex-husband. So I didn't sing in public; I rarely sang at home or even alone. I have conditioned my mind to believe I cannot sing. However, this is an untested theory because at moments of feeling free to express myself, I can actually hold a note. I simply have not held the belief that I can sing. To overcome this, I now sing whenever I can, but still only alone. A small goal I possess is to book myself in for singing lessons and to find out what type of voice I have. I know it's in there, but I have not yet crossed that bridge to find out. I still do not possess the confidence to book the lessons, but since it's a goal, I know I will.

We condition ourselves to believe what we are told from an early age. That is why I repeat daily to my children that they can 'be and do whatever they want'. I correct them when they say *I can't* or other negative phrases, and they often correct me when my old paradigms kick my butt! It's an on-going process of self-development. Remember these lyrics from that Billy Ocean song, 'When the going gets tough, the tough get going'? So keep going towards your dream despite the doubts created by your old, negative thought patterns; just keep going.

'To get through the hardest journey, we need take only one step at a time, but we must keep on stepping.'

~ Scottish Proverb

Why People Quit

There will always be a reason to quit. We can come up with so many valid and justifiable reasons to give up on our goals. In order to pursue our dreams, we sometimes have to let go of that which no longer serves us and that can be painful and create resistance in us. That's when we have to ask the question - is it necessary? Ask ourselves *is it necessary for me to keep going despite the struggle? Is my goal worth the effort?*

The correct answer? Yes. Yes it is! So don't give up; keep going!

Let's take a look at some of the reasons why people quit.

1. Criticism from Others

There will always be naysayers and doubters. When you start to shine bright, the other dull pennies around you will see the difference in you. That will attract two types of characters towards you: your supporters and your doubters. Ask yourself who you are going to listen to; those that support your dreams, vision or goals, or those that knock you down? Ask yourself why they criticise your dreams and ambitions. It can be challenging when the criticism or warnings come from loved ones or close friends, the very people you expect to support you. Don't judge them harshly though, as most of their doubts are personal and fear based. They also care about you and want the best, so their concern may be born out of genuine care and love for you.

These are a selection of possible reasons why others may criticise you and try to deflate your dreams.

- You are levelling up and they feel threatened
- They feel regret at not pursuing their own dreams
- It highlights their own unfulfilled potential
- They are full of fear
- They may be over protective

If receiving criticism or feeling the rejection and lack of support from others in the pursuit of your dreams is causing you to doubt yourself, take heart from this quote from Confucius:

'The superior man is distressed by the limitations of his ability; he is not distressed by the fact that men do not recognise the ability that he has.'

2. They Give Up Too Early

"If I quit now I will be back to where I started, and when I started, I was desperately wishing to be where I am now.'

~ Author Unknown

If you quit now, you will never know what may have been. Success may have been just around the corner. Why give up now when you are so close? If you give up, you may struggle for a long time with regret and disappointment in yourself. Don't fall in the trap of *'if only'* or *'what if'*. You've got this! You've come so far; keep pushing!

'Every great work, every great accomplishment, has been brought into manifestation through holding to the vision, and often just before the big achievement comes apparent failure and discouragement.'

~ Florence Scovel Shinn

3. Your Own Doubts and Fears

It's imperative you fight your own fears and doubts, and to fight any barriers and obstacles that come across your path. Failure, disappointment, doubt and pain are all normal on the path to achieving your dreams. It's in overcoming the struggle that we truly develop our character; we grow in the darker spaces. Fear of failure and fear of success are the two main fears on our way to becoming successful. In her book 'The Game of Life and How to Play It', Florence Scovel Shinn writes,

'Success is not final, failure is not final; it is the courage to continue that counts.'

4. You Made a Mistake or You Failed

It's okay to make mistakes and to fail. If a baby gave up learning to walk after the first time it fell down, human beings would possibly never have learned to walk. It takes courage and perseverance to keep trying, to get up after failure or making a mistake. Keep trying!

'In the midst of chaos, there is also opportunity.'

~ Sun Tzu, Philosopher

5. You Suffered Rejection

Everyone suffers rejection at some point in their lives. How we respond to rejection is the key to our success. Motivational speaker Les Brown says that every no brings us closer to a yes. See rejection as merely a re-direction and a necessary part of the process to achieving the success you want. Don't take rejection personally; learn from it and continue moving forward.

'...we rejoice in our sufferings, because we know that suffering produces perseverance; perseverance, character; and character, hope.'

~ Romans 5: 3-4

Why Not to Quit

'Great people are not affected by each puff of wind that blows ill. Like great ships, they sail serenely on, in a calm sea or a great tempest.'

~ George Washington, 1st President of the United States

Sometimes, though, it would be so easy to quit, right? To go hang up those boots which are tired from trudging continuously through the mire and the grunge. Yet we have to make that decision to keep moving; to keep going forward and not quit on ourselves and on our dreams, goals and ambitions.

Let's take a look at the reasons to keep going rather than to stop and quit on those dreams.

Trust the Process

The road to change and to becoming a better, more successful you is a process. It takes time to change and the bigger the goal, the longer the road. Think how long it's taken you to get to where you are today. Change isn't usually an overnight process; it takes many steps and some of those may feel like they are heading backwards rather than forwards. It takes time to realise a dream and achieve a goal. As the saying goes, Rome wasn't built in a day. In fact, it took one thousand years to build Rome. It should take you a lot less time to achieve what you want to achieve!

Philosopher Pluto wrote,

'As the builders say, the larger stones do not lie without the lesser.'

Trust Yourself

Do the work, take the advice, follow the steps outlined in this book and learn to trust in your own abilities. You have all the answers inside you. You have the power, the tools and the capabilities to achieve your goals, so do not let your lack of confidence in yourself, create barriers to realising your potential. Believe in you and trust yourself. I love this quote by the Dalai Lama:

'If you think you are too small to make a difference, try sleeping with a mosquito.'

When life knocks you down, it is sometimes difficult to get back up. It is hard to let go of pain and the old patterns of feeling like a victim. Painful memories are like the shadows of past ghosts, lingering and infesting our thoughts with the pain of wounds and bruises from yesteryear.

Letting go of old wounds and stepping into our destiny and living in the now to create a better future of ourselves is the greatest decision we can make towards the realisation of our dreams. Living your life in a victim mentality state is like being a dream thief. If you want to live a life that is free and full of new opportunity, then it is necessary to let go of past hurts. It is time to trust the process and to truly trust in yourself.

'When I let go of what I am, I become what I might be.'

~ Lao Tzu

You Will Learn Who You Are on Your Journey

This is so true, because it's in the challenge, the adversity and the struggle to overcome that we truly find out who we are and what we are made of. There is a saying that most of us have heard since childhood: 'Good things come to those who wait'. Be patient and trust in the process. Everything takes longer than you think, especially if it's a challenging goal you have set for yourself. You are on a journey and in order to stay focused on the path ahead, you need to keep your eyes on the goal.

'Mastering others is strength, mastering yourself is true power.'

~ Lao Tzu

Don't Be a Victim

Most of us struggle with having a victim mentality at some stage in our lives. Recognise this is where you once lived, and then let it go. Refuse to remain a victim and choose to be a winner instead. This is a key characteristic of becoming a highly successful person; to let go of the past, stop thinking like a victim and accept a better future through the pursuit of your dreams, ambitions and goals.

It's Possible

Take the word 'impossible' and change it to 'I'm possible'. It's the same letters in the same sequence, but the latter takes a negative word and flips it to a positive. That's what you have to do when adversity strikes you down and the road seems too tough a journey; flip it to a positive. Change 'I can't' to 'I can' and 'I won't' to 'I will'. Change your perception and repeat the words over and over, 'It's possible'.

Motivational speaker Les Brown, whom I refer to many times, has a speech that I often play on YouTube called 'It's possible'. I urge you to listen to it. Many times when I have felt close to quitting on my goals and dreams, or when a situation I faced seemed too difficult, I tune into this speech and repeat over and over his words, *'It's possible'*. Because it is, it **IS** possible. Do not quit on your dreams; merely change your perception and outlook on the situation.

It's Okay to Be You

Be yourself; be unique. Follow those who have already walked the path you are on and achieved success, but be yourself in the process and retain your individuality. You are your main selling point, so the more work you do on developing yourself into the person you want to become, the more others will believe in you and your vision. It's okay to be different from the pack; remember that leaders have to stand out from the crowd to be noticed. If you are the only person left believing in you, then that's enough. Lao Tzu wrote,

'When you are content to be simply yourself and don't compare or compete, everybody will respect you.'

Hang Around With Positive People

Remember that you are the sum total of the five people you hang around with (author Jim Rohn) so ensure that those people have got your back, support your dreams, are going in the same direction as you and enrich your life as opposed to draining you. Find mentors and coaches who share the same vision as you and follow those who have achieved success in the field you are journeying towards.

What Are You Reading, Listening to, and Watching?

Your reading material should be helping you to become a better you. Read at least ten pages of a self-development or inspirational book daily, or listen to these books on Audible or CDs. Tune in to motivational and inspirational teachers and speakers such as Lisa Nichols, Les Brown, Brene Brown, Oprah, Esther Hicks, Earl Nightingale, and Dr Wayne Dyer, to name but a few. This is my go-to list, but you can create your own. I call them my invisible mentors – they inspire me daily, yet they aren't even aware of my existence.

I rarely watch television and even more rarely purchase a newspaper. That doesn't mean I am ignorant to what is going on in the world, as there are other ways of catching up on national and international affairs. It simply means that I am not absorbing potentially negative influences on a daily basis, thus in turn distracting me from creating a positive, can do attitude in my life. If your thoughts become things as the Law of Attraction says, then I choose to refrain from focusing on negative situations and influences by creating a positive, goal focused mindset. Focus on the good and filter out the negative.

Adopt a 'No Matter What' Attitude

Watch your language and choose your thoughts wisely. Use affirmations and mantras such as '*I can do this*', '*I am enough*' and '*It's possible*' to keep your focus. Be unstoppable, no matter what, and visualise your goal by keeping your eyes firmly fixed on the outcome. Never stop trying and never give up until you have hit a home run or crossed the finish line.

Recognise Your Negative Behaviour Patterns

When you find yourself falling into old habits and paradigms, acknowledge them, pull yourself back and let them go. You have new paradigms, beliefs and tools in your kit bag now, so open it and pull one out. Zap away those negative behaviour patterns and get back on track towards achieving your vision.

Believe in You and Develop Inner Strength

Nothing can stop you if you believe in *YOU* enough. Trust yourself, trust the process and trust your vision. Buddha said, *'Be a light unto you'*. To be truly successful, you have to develop an inner strength that will act as your core and carry you through the tough times.

Success is getting to the point of knowing who you are and trusting yourself in the process and trusting your inner truth. Inner strength is usually born through adversity, challenge and struggle. It is in those dark and low places in our lives that we gain a deeper understanding of who we are. At the time of struggle and adversity, a way out may not always be clearly visible, but know it is there. When you finally emerge from that difficult place, you will discover that your endurance muscles have developed and your inner strength, although tested, has deepened that much more. Pain is a lesson. Author and poet Maya Angelou said that rainbows always came after the storm. Acknowledge the lesson and move forward. As the ancient philosopher Aristotle said,

'It is in our darkest moment that we must focus to see light.'

Hope

Hope is incredibly powerful. Aristotle said, *'Hope is a*

waking dream.' Hope is a conscious decision and gives us freedom to connect to a higher discipline other than ourselves; be that God, a Divinity, the Universe or an energy force. However you choose to see that higher connection, hope is a conscious decision to create deeper understanding and awareness in our lives. It is a powerful, conscious intention.

Hope gives us strength and it is derived from an inner strength. It is like a battery pack of power inside of us that we switch on when we require an additional inner power source. It has infinite possibilities and possibility provides hope. An unknown future is a hopeful future, so it is positive to take risks and get out of your own way and take opportunities when they arise. It is also the opposite of hopelessness, which can lead to anxiety, stress and despair. Hope gives us the strength inside that we require to create the change we are looking for in our lives.

'Were it not for hope, the heart would break.'

~ Scottish Proverb

Fall Down and Get Back Up Again

We all fall, we all fail and we all get despondent at times. What differentiates between a successful person and a non-successful person is that they get up time and time again, no matter what. Think of a boxer. Do they quit after they lose a match or get knocked down or out? I'm sure some might have done, but the common mentality of a boxer is that they keep fighting. They are taught that if they get knocked down, they get back up again, and again, and again.

They prepare themselves both mentally and physically for

the fight. They train and build up endurance. They keep their eyes on the prize. Sometimes they will win a fight and sometimes they will lose, but they will keep their eyes firmly fixed on the goal they have set for themselves. There will be small wins on the way to their destination goal, and each win is one step closer to their dream. This is the mentality we need to adopt to become successful and achieve our goals, vision and dreams. It's your goal and it's worth fighting for, so put on your imaginary boxing gloves and fight your doubts, lack of confidence, lack of belief and the naysayers and celebrate the small wins as they bring you one step closer to success.

'When you feel like quitting, think about why you started.'

~ Anonymous

~~~~~~~~~~~

A final note on this chapter - when I was a child I had the desire to one day become a writer. When I was twenty-five I wrote my first book and sent it to around twenty-three publishers. I suffered rejection after rejection and I quit. Twenty-five years later, I am getting my first (of many planned) poetry books published and, of course, this book. There are novels half written to follow.

If I hadn't given up all those years ago, if I had persevered instead of quitting on my dream of becoming a writer when I suffered rejection, where might I have been today? **So do not quit**. Keep going despite the rocky road, for it's in the struggle that we truly find out who we are.

'Everything in the Universe is inside you, ask all from yourself.'

~Rumi

Chapter Summary

1. Don't quit!
2. Paradigm and paradigm shift
3. Reasons why people quit
4. Reasons why you should not quit
5. When the going gets tough the tough stick it out!

Case Study 14: Philip Chan – Don't Quit

It is very easy to believe that if we keep trying we will succeed. However, that is simply not the case! Sure, in anything worthwhile, we need effort and persistence to make it happen and an attitude like the poem below:

When faced with a mountain

I will not quit.

I will keep on striving

Until I climb over,

Find a pass through.

Tunnel underneath,

Or simply stay and

Turn the mountain

Into a gold mine!

With God's help!

I am a very determined person and I did not quit at one business for over 10 years. I was working hard, very hard every week, but with little or no result - it was sensible to let it go and start a new business, which I did and in 4 months. I was working less and making more than I had in 10 years !

I am not a quitter but the saying "Insanity is doing the same thing over and over again and expecting a different result" was ringing so loud in my ear, I said to myself: " STOP!"

I had to take a hard look at the "system" I was using: it was wrong!

It is said that human nature will tolerate a level of pain and will not change, even when they know they should.

This could be anything in life: habits, relationships, etc. It is only when the pain becomes so unbearable, that we will take action rather living in false hope!

People who work hard can still go broke. Don't work hard; work smart first and then hard if necessary.

Smart, rich, successful people don't have to work hard if they have learnt to work smart!

Some of the wealthiest people in the world do not have any university degrees.

They earn in one day what takes most of us to earn working 40 hours a week, for over 40 weeks of the year, for over 40 years, then retiring at 40% of our full time income!

If you are flying and you are 1 degree off course at the start and you continue on that path, you will be hundreds, if not thousands of miles away from your final destination.

That was me!

You should not quit only if your goals are valid, well planned and realistic.

Constantly evaluate to make sure things are on track and if circumstances have not changed.

It is not so much as 'Don't quit' but act intelligently and be flexible.

Work hard when you need to, rest or do nothing sometimes, and give the process time or make the appropriate adjustments and 'Don't quit' on your dream and get other people involved to share the load. As John Paul Getty famously said,

"I would rather have 1% effort of 100 people then 100% of my own effort."

~ Philip Chan, Entrepreneur, Coach, Teacher, Mentor, Ten Seconds Maths Genius, Bodyguard

Case Study 15: Rachel – Don't Quit

Don't quit. Just don't. It's not an option. Well it is in a lot of cases, but not when it's your child battling her demons, who is crying out for help and no one is listening. Who will help her if I quit? Not her father who takes a holiday for two weeks during one of her breakdowns. Not the health professionals who lose patience with her self-destruction. Not the social workers who are just filling in their forms. Not the school that has her in isolation because she was considered a danger to other pupils by a psychologist who had never even met her! Not the police who let out her attacker on bail. Not the Crown Prosecution Service who decide to believe her groomer. Just me. Mum.

But that's what we do, us mums. Particularly us single mums. Her father quit 17 years ago when she was barely 2 years old. That's what some fathers do; they just go. They opt for that part-time parenting which is devoid of responsibility. For me, that isn't parenting, that is quitting. So why haven't I quit?

Because through everything that has happened, all I want for her is to be okay and for her to have her life back. I have put my life on hold for her to get hers back. That's what us mums do.

I cry myself to sleep at night, but in the morning I show up. I put on my face when I see her. I hold her when she needs me to. I leave when she asks to be alone, but I will never quit. I was put on this earth to get her through this. I'm Mum. I'm the one she can count on.

All the little worries that people have are brushed aside when you're in crisis. All you can think of is the next minute, the next hour, the next day. And that's why you don't quit.

Because one day will come a day better than the previous one. One day your child will smile. One day she will want to get dressed. One day she will leave hospital and you will be there to take her home. One day she will step onto a stage and you will cry because you didn't quit and she is here. And she is looking at her future.

~ Rachel, Business Owner and Mother of Three

SUMMARY

My hope is that you have picked up some tips, tricks, tools and techniques after reading this book and maybe a few golden nuggets too? I also hope you managed to do some of the suggested exercises and have scribbled and made notes throughout the pages.

Change is not easy and there will be times when getting to the space you want to be from the place you are now feels like a lifetime away from where you are standing/sitting. It's a process and sometimes the steps are gigantic and sometimes they feel tiny and inconspicuous. But they are there. Each step forward, no matter how small, is a step in the right direction.

To help you, I am summarising a daily to do list, or DMO – a daily method of operation. It may help you to process your steps towards achieving what you want and where you want to be.

This is optional, but I am putting it in here anyway. If it helps just one person, then it's worth it!

DAILY METHOD OF OPERATION (DMO)

From waking...

- Gratitude to reduce the feeling of sadness and lack
- Meditation to centre yourself
- Affirmations to affirm your goals/your vision/keep you directed
- Mirror work – to build self-love and self-appreciation
- Visualise where you would like to be or what you would like to do/have

Throughout the day...

- Watch your language
- Watch your thoughts
- Check your fears
- Step out of your comfort zone and get out of your own way
- Say yes and figure out the how later
- Be kind to you
- Know you are good enough
- Adopt a determined, 'no matter what' attitude to achieving your goals

Before bed...

- Gratitude for the small wins
- List or journal the positives and the successes, no matter how small
- Read your goals
- Affirmations
- Visualisation of your one big goal

Have fun with this and never quit. No matter where you are on your journey to self-improvement, there will always be roadblocks and barriers. Step over the stumbling blocks and work your way through the challenges. Trust the process and most importantly trust yourself. And no matter what, DO NOT QUIT!

Now go back and re-score your self-love mark in Exercise 4 from Chapter 2. Congratulate yourself if you moved up just one notch on the score; you are on your way! And keep walking this path, it's worth it!

AFTERWORD

It was one day in late August, I was lying in hospital after a near fatal cycling accident, thinking, 'I'm still alive, my brains still working, so who can I help?' I love helping people become a better version of themselves. My intuition had a feeling Paula was in need of some guidance and even though we had never met or even knew each other very well, she replied soon after I messaged her, saying that she would like my help. She explained her story, a struggling mother of three, and Paula was wanting to make changes in her life, achieve more and be an inspiration to her kids. This was perfect as this challenge was just what I was looking for.

I made the simple decision that I would help Paula, but only if she went on to help others after my services had been carried out, which she was happy to do. This book, I am sure, will be a testament to her journey and be full of tools and guidance that will help you through your journey also. As a coach and mentor, I had my work cut out in the beginning, breaking through barriers and limiting beliefs. Paula wanted her new life in six weeks; perhaps it was possible, but we had a lot of inner work to do. We went deep, which took time, but also created new beliefs, values and brought with it new opportunities.

After two months, I explained we could stop where we were, or keep going. There comes a point where it's hard to go back to who you were and it gets tougher as you work through all your thoughts and beliefs and tap into your subconscious mind, where we mostly work on auto pilot. I've had clients cry and wish they'd never met me at this stage: it's after years of programming, from family, teachers, friends and partners and living life on repeat. But Paula kept going, ever keen to change and achieve.

Were there niggles? Yes. Was it tough? Yes. Did it hurt at times? Yes! Making big changes isn't easy, as I'm sure you'll find out as you read through this book and discover Paula's learning, struggles and her breakthroughs and as you start to look into your own personal self-development. There were many times that Paula would thank me for not giving up on her, but I couldn't; I could see the shifts and changes happening in her life regularly. Her thoughts and words were changing and it was after about three months I said, 'Look back to when we started, does your life look or sound anything like it was back then?' to which she said 'No'. Of course it didn't, and would she ever be able to go back there, with all the new tools and mindset she was now carrying? No way.

There was breakthrough after breakthrough and a time came when I said to Paula to just say 'yes' to every opportunity she'd been presented with and we could talk over the things she wasn't sure of. Paula inevitably started meeting people, getting jobs abroad - including in TV and music as a makeup artist - and even applied to take part in a beauty contest. If you want to achieve anything great, you got to step out of your comfort zone, you got to have goals that scare the crap out of yourself sometimes. Paula prepared

herself for the beauty contest physically and mentally and had to speak publicly about herself in front of an audience; she totally smashed it and only went and won an award at the show. It truly was a turning point in Paula's life.

We would speak almost every day during my recovery, which helped to keep me focused on healing. My mind was occupied on seeing Paula achieve, working as a makeup artist, networking continuously, listening and reading her poetry and seeing her paint angels.

I loved hearing amazing new stories and seeing a continuous change in confidence. Where there's a will, there surely is a way.

I've watched Paula's values and beliefs change constantly. I like to describe the journey as time travel: you can be in the same spot for many, many years and in the space of six weeks, be in a completely different space. Paula's description and belief of success has changed since we started working together. Success doesn't necessarily need to be all about making money; you can be highly successful by just doing the things you love and in my opinion, that's where the money lies. I felt blessed to have been asked to write the foreword for this book; one of Paula's goals was of course to write books and be a public speaker.

I know you'll enjoy reading Paula's first book, full of tools and knowledge. It will make you think, help improve your life and bring you happiness, and I wish you all the very best on your journey. Well done, Paula!

With love,

Richard Marchand
richardtransforms@gmail.com

ACKNOWLEDGMENTS

At the end of the book, I have listed many authors and their books that have walked the journey with me, albeit as silent observers. My gratitude, in particular, for silent mentors such as Oprah, Les Brown, Maya Angelou, Dr Wayne Dyer, Tony Robbins and Lisa Nichols. Through their books, online videos and podcasts, I have listened, learned and gleaned so much invaluable advice and knowledge. I have walked in their light and absorbed their wisdom. I am truly grateful for all their knowledge and the courage for writing their journeys and thoughts down on paper and on video, to help others like me. They were called to do so, as I have been called to do so for you. That's part of my purpose: to survive my journey, heal from the pain and guide others going through theirs. I strongly encourage you to seek out mentors and coaches like these and learn from those who have walked the same path you hope to tread.

The majority of the quotes have been taken from the wisdom of ancient Chinese philosophers, alongside the Dalai Lama and quotes from some of my favourite actors and actresses. We can all learn so much from others' wisdom.

I am so grateful to many people who stayed with me or held my hand and lifted me up during my troubled years. Sara Martin, my best friend, for loving me as a sister and never walking away despite not knowing what to do with me half the time! Isabel Morris, friend and amazing poet, for encouraging my poetry writing and for loving me even in my darkest of spaces. Allie Kay for keeping me company on the phone every day of the writing process during weeks of isolation in lockdown. Thank you to all of you amazing women. I love you dearly. And finally to my friend Ceilia, for seeing in me what I couldn't see. I see it now

There are two people I really want to thank publicly, though, for helping change my mindset from lost in negative to bursting with positive. Richard Marchand, my life coach and friend. What an incredible person. He saw how trapped my soul was and helped me unglue myself from a mentally stuck place of old paradigms and destructive, negative thought patterns. I am forever grateful.

Finally, Ann Varney, healing hypnotherapist and spiritual healer. She tapped into my dark places and brought light. The sense of failure I carried and the depths of contorted emotion she saw and swept away with (more than a few) strokes of her healing ways. Plus the wonderful group of new friends in Scotland she introduced me to. Ann, you help so many people, including broken children and teens, and bring light and freedom to so many. You are an amazing person.

To all my friends, including Richard and Ann, thank you, thank you and thank you. And to you dear reader, for picking up this book and choosing it from the sea of others with a similar message, thank you for allowing me into your life. I truly hope you gain as much from my words as I have benefitted from the lessons that brought me here to you. Finally, here are words from my favourite film of all time:

'Strange, isn't it? Each man's life touches so many other lives.'

~ Clarence the Angel, It's a Wonderful Life

Much love, Paula Love Clark

APPENDIX

- Dr. Mary D. Moller, DNP, ARNP, PMHCNS-BC, CPRP, FAAN, associate professor and coordinator of the Psychiatric-Mental Health Doctor of Nursing Practice program at Pacific Lutheran University School of Nursing, Tacoma, Washington. Interview on the affects of fear on the mind and body.

- Jim Carrey, actor - Commencement Address speech at the 2014 Maharashi Graduation Ceremony (YouTube)

- Jack Canfield's video online - 'How To Overcome the Fears You Create' (May 2018)

- Dr Masara Emoto water experiment research 'The Hidden Messages in Water' published in 2004

- Carol Dweck, fs blog 2015 'A Summary of Growth and Fixed Mindsets'

- 'Disrupt Yourself: Putting the Power of Disruptive Innovation to Work' by Witney Johnson (2015 Amazon)

- 'Disruptors: Success Strategies From Women Who Break The Mold' by Dr Patti Fletcher (2018 Amazon)

- 'The Secret' by Rhonda Byrne (2006 Atria Books Beyond Words Publishing)

- 'Mirror Work: 21 Days to Heal Your Life' by Louise Hay (Hay House)

- 'How To Heal Your Life' by Louise Hay (Hay House)

- 'The Structure of Scientific Revolutions' by Thomas Khun (1962 University of Chicago Press)

- 'The Power of Intention' by Dr Wayne Dyer (Hay House)

- No Matter What' by Lisa Nichols (Hachette UK, 2010)

- 'Feeling Is The Secret' by Neville Goddard (1944)

- 'The Strangest Secret' online speech by Earl Nightingale (1957)

- 'It's Possible' YouTube speech by Les Brown

- Richard Marchand life coach – richardtransforms@gmail.com

- Ann Varney spiritual coach – www.annvarney.com / email annvarney@outlook.com

Printed in Great Britain
by Amazon

41753163R00154